Praise for *STEM, STEAM, M...*

"*STEM, STEAM, Make, Dream* is Dr. Chris Em... unapparelled work of art does what many texts s... ...y cannot do. It tells us what to do, explains why it will work, and empowers the reader to teach STEM in a way that will transform generations of learners. This is *THE* text for every science teacher training program and professional development."

—Bryan A Brown, PhD, professor of science education, Stanford University

"I have so much respect for Chris Emdin as an educator, visionary, and challenger-of-the-not-good-enough-status-quo. Like Chris, I believe that in so many ways, unnecessary obstacles have been put in the way of too many young people—particularly students of color. Yes, STEM and STEAM are for everyone. Who better than Chris to help us get there."

—Angela Duckworth, professor of psychology at the University of Pennsylvania, cofounder and CEO of Character Lab, author of *Grit*

"In *STEM, STEAM, Make, Dream*, Christopher Emdin has stitched together an educational quilt where each piece tells a powerful story. You don't have to be engaged in STEM or even in the education profession to enjoy and learn from the powerful stories told in this volume. It is a wonderful, must-read!"

—Gloria Ladson-Billings, professor emerita at the University of Wisconsin–Madison, president of the National Academy of Education (2018–2021), author of *The Dreamkeepers*, *Critical Race Theory in Education*, and *Culturally Relevant Pedagogy*

"In *STEM, STEAM, Make, Dream*, Chris Emdin offers a decisive call to action: to break down barriers to STEM fields and the arts—especially for Black, Brown, and Indigenous children—by seeing and celebrating the curiosity and creativity that make children natural problem solvers, scientists, mathematicians, innovators, artists, builders, and dreamers. With clarity, wit, and timely examples, Dr. Emdin calls on both educators and caregivers to identify and dismantle harmful and exclusionary patterns that often pervade STEM, and to create new relationships with STEAM fields. His vision, articulated in this powerful book, will support the promise of the brilliant children in our homes, classrooms, and communities as they dream into existence a more beautiful and liberated world."

—Deborah Loewenberg Ball, William H. Payne Collegiate
Professor of Education at the University of Michigan, Arthur F.
Thurnau Professor, and the founding director of TeachingWorks.

"A compelling, ground breaking, accessible, and timely take on the problems in STEM education and how we can improve it. The powerful stories and perspectives here will usher in a new way of thinking and a new generation of STEM professionals."

—Stephon Alexander, professor of physics, Brown
University; Author of *Fear of a Black Universe: An
Outsider's Guide to the Future of Physics*

Christopher Emdin

With contributions from
**Tasnim Aziz, Stephanie Pearl,
and Neal Schick**

Original Illustrations by Johann Hauser-Ulrich

STEM, STEAM, MAKE, Dream

Reimagining the Culture of Science, Technology, Engineering, and Mathematics

International Center for
Leadership in Education.

From Houghton Mifflin Harcourt.

International Center for Leadership in Education, Inc
1587 Route 146
Rexford, New York 12148
www.LeaderEd.com
info@LeaderEd.com

ISBN: 978-1-328-03428-1

International Center for Leadership in Education is a division of Houghton Mifflin Harcourt.

Printed in the United States of America.

1 2 3 4 5 6 7 8 9 10   7239   30 29 28 27 26 25 24 23 22 21

4500841688 ABCD

Cover images: Music icon © Alamy/Subhan Baghirov, planet icon © Alamy/Freud, shoe icon © Alamy/Elcan Huseynaliyev, map icon © Alamy/Oleksandr Drypsiak, compass icon © Alamy/Oleksandr Drypsiak, computer icon © Alamy/Qalib Abiyev, graph icon © Alamy/Christian Horz, test tubes icon © Alamy/studicon, gear icon © Alamy/Flat Art, tools icon © Alamy/Maryna Bahrovska, solar icon © Alamy/Idalba Granada, spray can icon © Alamy/studicon, trumpet © Alamy/studicon, Pi icon © Belle Design, Galaxy background © DigitalVision Vectors

Interior images: Little Miss Flint © REUTERS / Alamy Stock Photo, Cornrow Curves © Ron Eglash, GZA © Chris Blizzard / Alamy Stock Photo, Shoe blueprint © Jeffery Alan Henderson, Janani Balasubramanian © Kelle Cruz, STEAM © Freepik, Foldit protein © Brian Koepnick / University of Washington, Sajid Iqbal © Sadek Hossain Munna, Raven Baxter © Raven Baxter, Victoria Richardson © Victoria Richardson, Outdoor Classroom © DownCity Design, Paper Modeling © Girls Garage, Ayanna Howard © John Amis/AP Images for HMH, Michael Kobrick © Photographer Unknown/AP images for HMH, George Washington Carver © Everett Collection Inc/Alamy, Elvia Niebla © J. Michael Short/AP Images for HMH, N. Christina Hsu © Nick Wass/AP Images for HMH, Thomas Edison © Archive Pics/Alamy, Claudia Alexander © Phil McCarten/AP images for HMH, Chris Emdin, © Chris Emdin

Contents

Volume 1
STEM

VOLUME 2
STEAM

APPENDIX

ACTIVITIES

NOTES

About the Author

DR. CHRISTOPHER EMDIN is the Naslund Endowed Chair in Curriculum and Teaching and Professor of Education at the University of Southern California. He was previously a professor of science education at Teachers College, Columbia University, and is one of the nation's leading voices on equity in education. Chris is the founder of Science Genius and author of the *New York Times* bestseller *For White Folks Who Teach in the Hood . . . and the Rest of Y'all Too* and *Ratchetdemic: Reimagining Academic Success*. His work has appeared in the *Atlantic*, the *Wall Street Journal*, and the *Washington Post*.

About the International Center for Leadership in Education

THE INTERNATIONAL CENTER FOR LEADERSHIP IN EDUCATION (ICLE), a division of Houghton Mifflin Harcourt, challenges, inspires, and equips leaders and teachers to prepare their students for lifelong success. At the heart of all we do is the proven philosophy that the entire system must be aligned around instructional excellence—rooted in rigor, relevance, and relationships—to ensure that every student is prepared for a successful future.

Founded in 1991 by Dr. Bill Daggett, ICLE, through its team of thought leaders and consultants, partners with schools and districts to implement innovative practices to scale through professional learning opportunities guided by the cornerstones of our work: the Daggett System for Effective Instruction® and the Rigor/Relevance Framework®. In addition, ICLE shares successful practices that have a positive impact on student learning through keynote presentations, the Model Schools Conference, and a rich collection of publications. Learn more at LeaderEd.com.

Introduction

SCHOOL WAS NOT DESIGNED for him to love science, math, or related subjects. Frankly, neither was home. This is not to say there wasn't love, belief, rigor, or motivation at home. It is to say that words like *scientist* or *mathematician* weren't said out loud in reference to him. He never felt them in the air, never breathed them in. They were simply unsaid. Words unsaid find a way to create a fracture in one's sense of self. They linger in the heart and mind, then find a way to shatter visions of who you are or who you think you can be. They shape who you are even more when you know the words exist, but just not for you.

These words that are unsaid—the words that don't exist for you—shape your identity even more than the words you hear.

He heard words like *funny* and *artistic*. Phrases like "You can draw well, and I like what you wrote." The words he heard somehow made him strong, but they made no space for words like *math* and *science* to make a home within him. The words that were never used to describe him danced in his mind and chipped away at his STEM identity. In school he heard phrases like "You can't do science" and "Math is hard for a lot of people." These phrases—and the looks that came with them—set him on a course away from STEM and, in many ways, away from school.

The course was intricate, though, as the young man still found ways to love STEM (an acronym for **s**cience, **t**echnology, **e**ngineering, and **m**ath). It just was never named or attributed to him. He loved building things and measuring how tall they could get. He tinkered with toys so often that he didn't get to play with them because they always ended up with their insides sprawled across the floor. Cars turned into springs, wires, and batteries . . . and the word *destructive* came way before scientist, engineer, or mathematician. In fact, he didn't hear those words until after high school, four years of dodging math and science classes while searching for places where the "things he was good at" could cloak him from all the "you cannots" that were attached to being scientific or mathematical. Instead, he drew. He joked. He rapped. Rapping was important. It let him write words in rhyme; it allowed him to perform and express an identity that the world had shaped for him. Angry. Loud. Unafraid.

After years of being shaped and unshaped by what he heard—and didn't hear—he stumbled into college. Literally stumbled. He faltered into a fight in high school, tripped over a suspension during his senior year, watched his high school graduation ceremony slip right between his fingers, and fell into a local college a fifteen-minute walk from home. His intention was to major in "something to do so my folks wouldn't think I was completely useless."

After weeks of carving out a course schedule that had loose parameters, but a strict self-imposed boundary at anything science or math related, he walked into the mandatory meeting with a campus advisor.

"What do you want to major in?" the advisor asked.

He shrugged. "I'm still figuring it out, but not anything with science."

A suggestion from the advisor shifted everything. "You have to take science and math to graduate. One strategy is to get them out of the way now and then you don't have to worry about them later."

It made sense: suffer now and be free later. He decided to take Introduction to Biology.

The biology lecture hall looked and felt like all the other classrooms he had attended thus far. The only difference was the air. The air in the hall was thick. The kind of air "smart" people breathe. He settled into a seat all the way in the back of the classroom. Not back and center, either. Back and all the way to the left, next to the windows so he could have something to look at and be as far away as possible from the professor, who soon arrived.

She was white and wore glasses. She reminded him of all the other science teachers he had met before. She told the class her name, then rambled through something about biology, life, and its importance. She then started talking about her research. She spoke about something related to cells, brains, and schizophrenia.

Turning away from the windows and back to the class, he found that his interest was somewhat piqued.

She mentioned that she had a spot for a student who was interested in doing some biology research FOR FREE. Who would want to work for free? How much more boring would a science laboratory be than a science classroom? At some point, after half listening during the class and considering whether it was too late to drop it, the young man heard someone in the class mention that anyone who works in the lab gets extra credit.

This grabbed his attention. From the moment he signed up for the class, he knew he would need extra credit. For him, extra credit in school had never been about doing more. It had always been about catching up. Now, in a college science class, he knew he had to catch up before he even got started.

For his first day working in the lab, he put on his special outfit. Baggy jeans, a brightly colored rugby shirt, and a scowl. The scowl was the most important part of the outfit. Without it, the outfit would be incomplete. It was needed to communicate confidence, convey self-assuredness, and mask feelings of self-doubt and inadequacy. He wore it to science and math classrooms and other places where he didn't feel welcome. Today, as he walked into an actual science lab, he found it absolutely necessary.

At first glance, the laboratory was a completely foreign and intimidating world. Elaborate equipment, people in white lab coats, a feeling of efficiency and purpose that made everyone seem as though they were important. He was offered a lab coat, and he thrust his arms right into it. No tests and no doubt that he had something to contribute. He received a quick overview of the lab and its goal, a description of all the tasks that had to be completed, and a question asking what he saw himself doing.

At one point, he noticed music playing in the background as folks did real science. He saw his peer scientists humming songs and tapping their feet as they worked. He saw enjoyment and smiles living in the same space as rigor and research. This wasn't about rote memorization or regurgitating information. It was about doing and enjoying the process. This is not to say there were no rules or structures, but the ones that were given were explained and made sense. The process of rigor did not mean the absence of joy or passion. In fact, creating joyous and passionate contexts came first, then the rigor grew from there—to make it irresistible.

This was the first time that he began making the associations between science and music that have become the structure of this book. Each chapter delves into an aspect of music production and becomes a way to articulate how we must begin with STEM and then improve engagement in it by expanding the ways to both teach it and teach about it.

PTSD—Poor Treatment in STEM Disorder

STEM and trauma are intimately connected because STEM has been built on the concept of exclusivity. STEM professionals are framed as having a rare intelligence, a distinct authority, and a reverence that regular folks do not have access to. Yet there is always a call for more STEM programs and talk of the need for more young people to engage in it. The exclusivity of STEM, the pushing of young folks away from STEM, and the concurrent and persistent call for more STEM workers make young people question what's actually true. *You say you need me, but you do not welcome me. You say I need STEM, but you do not make me feel like I am part of it.*

There is a hypocrisy that the STEM world creates, which feels schizophrenic for young people. That feeling is the trauma that STEM induces. It is a very particular form of PTSD. A *poor teaching of STEM disorder* and *poor treatment in STEM disorder* that get manifested as a distancing of self from these disciplines at best, and an outright phobia of these disciplines in far too many cases. The extent to which this phobia affects a wide swath of the population is evident in the fact that so many people across the country are not scientifically literate. They shy away from scientific conversations and make decisions that do not consider research or evidence. We are in a world where issues like the denial of climate change and the proliferation of misinformation about vaccines persist because basic scientific knowledge does not exist.

I argue that this is directly related to the fact that science is unapproachable.

It is my belief—one based on extensive experience—that STEM culture has created its own walls. It has been about memorization. It has been about charged questions, such as, Is a child smart enough? Motivated enough? Eager enough? Good enough at following rules and raising a hand? These dogmas have made STEM restricted and exclusionary, at a great cost to our children and our future.

But I want STEM back. I want it back for my students, your students, and all young folks. I want science, technology, engineering, and mathematics to be a part of every child's vocabulary, identity, and culture. In *STEM, STEAM, Make, Dream*, I want to provide you—and all educators—with the tools needed to speak truth to power, to reclaim STEM as part of our shared experience.

Many of the people who were interviewed for this book offer us a view into what STEM education could look like if we aimed for a more expansive approach to teaching those disciplines. They exist at intersections and margins, yet have found ways to make their STEM identities prominent along with all the other aspects of who they are. Their core selves aren't sacrificed for their STEM selves, and vice versa. They are astrophysicists, Nobel Prize winners, artists, rappers, and teachers. Each has a certain confidence and brilliance that invokes a powerful curiosity in me. I wanted to know how they have formed their lives. And most important, I wanted to glean from them insights into what we must do for the next generation. I engaged in deep listening to their stories and special moments. In our interviews, they shared the moments that affirmed them and made them strong, but also the ones that were designed to break them. From this listening, I arrived at this work.

STEM, STEAM, Make, Dream is about removing obstacles—or at least pointing out where the obstacles are on a young person's journey. The book is about how to get over, under, and around metaphorical and actual barriers. This work is not about describing the history of STEM or of STEAM. It is not a deep dive into historical facts or a rehashing of existing perspectives from those who seek to maintain the power these disciplines hold. If you are looking for an in-depth examination of how best to teach science or math as it currently exists, please look elsewhere.

Instead, *STEM, STEAM, Make, Dream* is my attempt to reveal the truth about how we have excluded far too many people from the study, opportunity, and, yes, joyous rigor of STEM and STEAM. This includes framing a path toward accessibility and possibility. Maybe most important, it is a perspective on teaching to create full, whole, strong STEM-immersed young people who can maintain the scientist and mathematician identity they came into the world with before school, society, and words, both said and unsaid, chipped away at their natural inclination to be STEM superheroes.

To be clear, this is not a deep dive into the four disciplines that make up STEM. Instead, it is a guided tour through what I like to think of as the STEM neighborhood, as depicted in the *STEM, STEAM, Make, Dream* map at the beginning of the book. I go into greater detail on how the STEM neighborhood is designed, with coordinating streets and a local language, in chapter 1. For now, I just want you to think of STEM as an inclusive place that honors all cultures, aesthetics, and identities.

I think of STEM as the perfect hip-hop song. It requires digging into what has been done in the past to find what resonates in the present (digging in), identifying the best aspects of the classics and incorporating them into the work being currently done (sampling), creating something succinct that connects the past to the present (finding a bassline), understanding fundamental principles that tie complex ideas together (adding a drumbeat), being innovative in what is added to what exists (adding the sprinkles), creating a structure or frame for the work being engaged in (laying out song steps), putting ideas on paper or written form to be captured and edited (drafting the verse), perfecting what has been written or documented to shared (growing the rhyme), putting all that work together in a way that makes sense to you (laying the track), and then distributing the work to the public in a way that is palatable to a wide audience (mixing and mastering). This is what makes a perfect song and it is what makes a place that welcomes all.

A Neighborhood Map for All

To help all children claim their STEM identity, *STEM, STEAM, Make, Dream* provides educators, policymakers, community leaders, and parents with tangible ways to honor culture, increase equity, and encourage curiosity For creators, innovators, scientists, and entrepreneurs. This includes providing the tools and knowledge necessary to advocate for sustainable change and to address inequity, apathy, and the many other real problems in education. For parents, the book demystifies STEM and shows a clear pathway to empowering children with the skills needed to succeed in a science- and tech-based world. In doing so, it will inspire parents, educators, and policymakers alike to rethink the very nature and purpose of STEM education.

Visually Rich, Easily Applied

STEM, STEAM, Make, Dream explores the ways that science, technology, engineering, and mathematics can transform ALL young people's lives through learning. This includes reimagining our collective relationship to STEM by presenting it as more accepting and accessible than previously acknowledged. Beginning with the ways that STEM has been used to marginalize many children, the book examines the need for the arts—including culture—to serve as an anchor for instruction. It also describes the need for "making" (hands-on creation and tinkering) in establishing relevance in learning. Then, through an experiential approach, the book articulates the value of dreaming of a future that is inclusive of all young people, especially those furthest from opportunity.

In exploring these four themes, the book combines real-world stories and inspiring biographies in a visually rich package that includes inspirational quotes and best practices. To help ground theory, readers will hear from—and be inspired by—practitioners, activists, and artists ranging from a renowned NASA astronaut to an award-winning chemist to a Grammy-nominated musician. In profiling these innovators, the book reveals how readers can nurture creativity, spark joy, and promote perseverance in all children. Other special features include the following:

- Chapter-ending takeaways
- Special elements throughout that profile STEM professionals or provide inspirational, real-world examples
- A STEM-STEAM glossary
- A sampling of practical activities to showcase creative ways these ideas can be easily implemented in any classroom

If you haven't already figured it out, that young man in the opening story was me. That very first day in the laboratory, wearing a borrowed lab coat and hoping to earn a few points of extra credit, I decided to major in biology. Months later, I decided that I could study both biology and chemistry. My introduction to science and STEM came not in my K–12 experience but because of a random set of coincidences. These coincidences have shaped not just my life experiences but my identity—the very essence of who I am. I went on to enjoy my experiences researching the etiology of schizophrenia so much that I studied physical anthropology, biology, and chemistry in college. I then completed a master's degree in natural sciences, conducting research on mesenchymal stem cells, and ultimately became a science teacher and a professor of science education.

The key point is this: the entire direction of my life shifted through an experience that made me see myself differently than ever before.

It is this experience—coupled with the recognition that I could have easily missed it if not for several coincidences, luck, and opportunities—that led me to write this book. I recognize that given my experiences from childhood through high school, the likelihood that I would have opted to pursue STEM was slim to none. The statistics support this; there is endless data that speaks to the fact that persistence in STEM for young people, and especially for young people who come from where I come from, is not commonplace. It is for this reason that *STEM, STEAM, Make, Dream* exists. I hope to ensure that the belief in self that is essential for even thinking of oneself as a scientist, mathematician, or engineer is a significant part of classrooms. That the seeds of this belief won't languish and die prematurely if not for a string of coincidences. I wrote this book to reframe and reimagine STEM teaching and learning so that it addresses the trauma that comes from words that weren't said at home and only said in immutable, veiled ways in school.

I believe that we are all born to be STEM people. As young children, we all think deeply, tinker, play, question, categorize, make meaning, interpret, and draw connections. We come into the universe inquisitive about all that is around us and have natural dispositions and leanings that are assigned to "STEM people," even though we all hold them. This inquisitiveness remains until we are enveloped by the schooling system, a system responsible for teaching us so much about the world, a system that too often trains us to let go of an identity that we all hold. It teaches us how to learn without recognizing that we already hold learning deep within us. It teaches us how to question, but often leaves us unable to ask the *right* questions. Schooling teaches us to unlearn how we intrinsically learn. My hope and goal with *STEM, STEAM, Make, Dream* is to restore and build on our natural inclinations to explore, discover, create, and imagine. This is a hope for all learners—teachers and students alike—and the goal is especially focused on building equitable opportunity in our schools, so that we all have access to strong identity-shaping, life-changing experiences.

STEM

CHAPTER 1

Digging in the Crates

STEM is not a collection of academic subjects. It is not a field of study or an approach to curriculum.

It is an idea.

STEM is a concept that has existed for a long time and that found greater relevance when it became a part of the public discourse in the early 2000s. This is not to say that pursuing STEM is a bad thing to do. Instead, it is to say that STEM holds a mystique that we must understand in order to engage with it. **S**cience, **t**echnology, **e**ngineering, and **m**athematics are individually powerful areas of study. STEM is a merging of the four for the sake of convenience, but not necessarily for utility. Each of the subjects that compose it are revered by the public because they help us make sense of or enhance our world. Bringing them together into a single entity coalesces their power, but also isolates them from the endless connections that exist with other worlds and subjects that help us make sense of the world. Disciplines such as history and language, for example, cannot be teased away from STEM. What we know and why we know it is directly informed by history. The way we identify what we study or create and the deep meanings behind them are intimately connected to our language. But these connections, however powerful, have no space in STEM as it is currently presented to the world.

Administrators at the National Science Foundation who popularized the term in the early 2000s presented it as an ideal to aspire to, a thing we have to do better at, and not as something that we already embody. STEM is perceived as a mythical place we must travel to, a height we must attain that resides far above us. Unless we change this framing, it will always be something out of reach for the general populace. The exclusivity that is part of STEM does not match the call for more people to engage in it. The narrative that it is only for the select few who have some unique gifts fails to account for the reality. ALL people come into the world with an innate STEM knowledge . . . and we all can enhance or develop the skills, traits, attributes, and dispositions that are necessary for building that knowledge. In fact, many employ what would be otherwise called STEM skills outside classrooms and laboratories every day. If our collective goal is to improve engagement with and participation in STEM, I suggest that we focus on the following three questions:

- How do we reimagine the ways we view people and their ability to engage in STEM?
- How do we develop a method or approach that focuses on identifying, harnessing, and transferring "non-STEM" skills toward the disciplines?
- How do we demystify STEM? How do we get rid of the random nonproductive exclusivity we attach to these disciplines?

In this process, we have to unravel the components of STEM from each other. For a moment, we must let science, technology, engineering, and mathematics stand alone. They are different streets that help make up a neighborhood, as loosely depicted in the book's opening illustration. Science is the main thoroughfare, simply because it comes first. It is the most ubiquitous of the disciplines. Science is everywhere and is everything. It is not a sum of the specializations such as neuroscience or astrophysics that associate themselves with it, but the discovery of a method for doing ANYTHING. Science is also the gradual fine-tuning of a way of doing or discovering things based on what has previously been done. Technology, the next street in the neighborhood, is believed to be a set of technical skills or knowledge that only few possess or can access. It is neither. It is simply the process of making things to improve the human experience or to make life easier. Sure, it gets more detailed as the machines we make—or instruct—get more complex and develop their own language. But at its core, technology is about making things that work for us so that we don't have to work as hard. Engineering, the next street in the neighborhood, is about how things work. It is a process of understanding, designing, and building informed by science and math. Mathematics is the language spoken in the neighborhood. Numbers are simply the letters of the language of mathematics. As is the case with any language, fluency is developed over time and with use. Math does not bar anyone from engaging with it. In fact, there are entry points for everyone who engages with it, and for those who do, they develop skills as they use them over time.

My intention here is not to be reductive or overly simplistic in my description of these subjects. It is to make clear that experts within them are simply those who have sat with them the longest. The four fields are grouped together because they are proximal to each other, not because they require more from us intellectually. People do well in STEM because it is the neighborhood they live in. You are familiar with the street that you live on and the neighborhood you are from because you have spent the most time there. Our work as educators—and citizens—is to bring other folks to the neighborhood and make it appealing enough for them to want to stay.

As in any neighborhood, there are always a number of streets that are close by that just don't fit because of arbitrary geographic boundaries. This is how the combining of science, technology, engineering, and mathematics has occurred. They just happen to sit within the neighborhood, so we start giving them a shared identity. That is a great neighborhood. That is a tough neighborhood. Those are challenging or rigorous subjects. It's all in the naming and the broad associations that are made by the public.

Nobel Prize winner in chemistry Joachim Frank, when asked about the grouping of STEM, took a deep breath, a thoughtful pause, and then said, "I don't really know. I don't know the background of how this whole merger of ideas occurred. You could say it is obvious. That maybe it has always been obvious why we suddenly talk about them as a cluster. I think maybe what is behind it is a move away from specialization and the fact that we're more global. The global picture has created an understanding of the interconnectedness of technologies and our knowledge base."

This powerful stance moves us to see STEM as a way of thinking that undergirds the disciplines, rather than as a set of practices. STEM then becomes more of a philosophical construct. When Frank talks about STEM being about interconnectedness, he takes us to a place of considering intangible phenomena that make us associate ideas and disciplines with each other. His stance moves me to think of STEM as a nod toward interdisciplinarity and not as a way to exclude other disciplines—as it has regrettably become. STEM comes together not to dismiss other disciplines but to put forth a model of thinking that is a first step toward where we need to be—investigating and exploring the connections among all disciplines.

STEM, in its current iteration, has absorbed an American history of rugged individualism and beating the competition. This is *not* what STEM itself is, but a reputation it has inherited from when the US was steeped in fear of being outpowered by the former Soviet Union after the launch of *Sputnik*, the world's first artificial satellite. This success of the former Soviet Union somehow invoked a feeling of inferiority that spurred on a need to prove ourselves as "better than" or "the best and brightest." The current focus on STEM has inherited that fear of being left behind, that desire to be the best and brightest—at the expense of those who we perceive are inferior. The reality is that when we position some as brilliant, we implicitly identify others as not. Too many young people just do not see themselves as scientists right now. This is because we have a narrow idea of smartness and intelligence, and we have attached that narrow view to STEM identity.

Deficit Lens—STEM Trauma

STEM ability is distributed evenly across the populace. STEM identity is created when that natural ability is fostered by human activity. We are at our very core scientific creatures, but we believe in our STEM selves when the world reinforces what we are. When you think about a baby being born, the very first set of knowledge they are using is scientific knowledge. They are smelling their environment and making observations in

"Schooling is the undoing of your innate STEM ability."

—Chris Emdin

the world. They are not using English. They are not using history. They are using math and science. They are making observations, identifying patterns, testing hypotheses, and drawing conclusions. Once they start associating language with what they are seeing, they start expressing what is unfolding before them. There is magic in that unleashing, that revealing. This process is the foundation of STEM. This is what we need to build on in classrooms. Unfortunately, it is not what contemporary STEM education focuses on.

Today, if we ask young people, STEM is not about giving voice or language to observations and questions. The only thing it unleashes or reveals is that it is hard and not for everybody. Hundreds of interviews I have held with young people from urban classrooms about science reveal that many students simply believe that "science is hard." Many of these students, particularly those who were not doing well in science or mathematics classrooms, also believe that the reason they are not doing well is that they are not "smart enough." This idea of the "hardness" of science and, by proxy, STEM, is important to deconstruct.

 For many, the hardness of STEM is associated with it being academically challenging and with folks not being able to engage with it. In reality, the hardness is about the inflexibility of STEM and the fact that it does not bend to the needs of the person engaging with it. If I attempt to engage with a topic and find it hard, I blame myself without considering that there is something about the subject that is unapproachable. The perception is that the fault cannot possibly be with the academic subject or the methods used to teach it. This flawed approach to thinking about STEM does not consider the more expansive view of the concept of hardness and the notion that if the subject bends to me or my interests, I can forge a relationship to it that increases my desire to spend more time with it. Time spent equals familiarity. And familiarity eventually equals fluency in the language of the "hard" subject. What is hard becomes malleable enough to wrap around you once you are familiar with the language it speaks.

Make no mistake: this is not an argument for making subjects easier or less rigorous. Instead, it is an argument for making STEM subjects easier to embrace. It is about recognizing the traumas we create when we convince otherwise intelligent people that there are subjects too mentally challenging for them. This misstep overshadows the real issue, which is that the subject was likely presented poorly, spilling over with meanings attached to words like *smart* or *hard.*

STEM-Based PTSD

I mentioned PTSD (post-traumatic stress disorder) in the introduction, and I often talk about it at conferences or in the classes I teach. This is a disorder that emerges after a person has experienced or witnessed a terrifying event that they cannot escape from. It causes intense emotional and physical reactions and, in many instances, negatively shapes the life of the person who experienced the trauma. The experiences of young people in STEM mirror those of people who suffer from PTSD. So much so, I would argue that there is a **poor teaching in STEM disorder** that is a function of a number of traumatic experiences in classrooms where young people are inundated with words and messages about their inferiority.

Young people are sent to school and told to work hard, listen to their teachers, and do well on assessments that test their knowledge or intelligence. In the process, they are told that their hard work is not transferrable across settings in the school or across classes. For example, young people often work very hard at play and discover that they are very good at the observing, reflecting, performing, and imagining involved in play. Most important, they are affirmed for their expertise in play from the friends they play with. When they leave the playground and walk into the classroom, especially the STEM classroom, they are told that playtime is over. The real work of learning science and math begins. Learning is then framed as the opposite of the intense play and discovery they just participated in. They are told that in the classroom, they need to start doing the very things they were just doing—focusing, being resilient, and working hard.

Confusing, right? This, of course, invokes a sense of bewilderment in the young person. *How can I stop doing what you asked while doing what you asked? How can I be who you want me to be while turning off who I am? How am I to do these things when I am being told that this is for the best and brightest and that I am not doing it well?* This begins the process of young people identifying themselves, often at a very young age, as "not a math person" or "not a science person." They associate the subjects with self-doubt and inadequacy. Each of the STEM classes becomes a location of trauma, and the subjects are avoided from early on in the lives of too many.

In this way, STEM is not just the bringing together of four subjects; it is the bringing together of fears and feelings of inadequacy. We are pulling together four types of trauma. We are connecting four areas of study that foster elitism and have developed a kind of exclusionary culture.

The elitism of "hard science" keeps kids away from STEM. To combat it, we must be intentional about marketing it differently. This requires an intentional countering of all the existing narratives that do not accurately reflect what it takes to do well in STEM—or to be STEM. If STEM culture has been about memorization and giving off an "Are you smart enough to be part of us?" narrative, then we must be explicit about the many counternarratives that prove that this way of thinking is more reflective of people's constructions about the disciplines than what is required to actually engage in them. Rather than tell stories of perfect and infallible STEM heroes, we need to narrate their real stories and lives. Stories of Einstein's bad grades and Galileo's persecution are more powerful in creating the next generation of STEM than the theory of relativity and the calculation of gravity.

Putting in Kids, Churning Out "Graduates"

In many ways, the current school system has been designed to squeeze out the creativity of students. Its infatuation with assessments that measure only a particular type of knowledge—and a singular way of expressing that knowledge—leads to teaching that functions only to support those assessments. Learning has been reduced to cramming for tests, and in this type of system, students are reduced to containers that hold knowledge, instead of creators of it. In STEM education, the instruction is even more restrictive than in other disciplines. Forms of intelligence other than what is labeled as the logical and mathematical (which I argue reduces mathematical intelligence to a shell of what it really is) are not only discouraged from being expressed but are assaulted when expressed. Kids are being deprived of what they need to grow intellectually. When they cannot question, create, critique, and be vocal or expressive in the STEM classroom, we must reimagine the process of STEM education to include these behaviors. This approach stands in contrast to an efficiency model of teaching that is about what is easiest to do to get the student ready for the assessment.

Mathematician Ron Eglash, whom I interviewed for this book, describes how such concepts as optimization, efficiency, and work output

STEM
INSPIRATION

Amariyanna "Mari" Copeny—Little Miss Flint

Widely known as Little Miss Flint, Mari Copeny is an activist from Flint, Michigan. Mari is known for raising awareness about Flint's water crisis, which lasted from 2014 to 2019. In 2016, when Mari was eight years old, she wrote a letter to President Barack Obama to increase awareness of the water crisis in her hometown. Her letter inspired the following response from the president: "Letters from kids like you are what make me so optimistic about the future." For more about Mari, visit her at https://www.maricopeny.com/.

The simple fact is, we must look at the outcomes of our existing practice and move in a radically new direction. If we do not like the product, we need to reimagine the process. If our school system is failing to create a population of young people who are proficient in and engaged in STEM, we must dig into, question, and interrogate the process of schooling.

have become staples in STEM and have now become part of STEM education. Chemical, agricultural, and even mathematical research asks questions about machine efficiency. How much power is necessary to get a weight lifted? And educators started looking at students as though they were products instead of people. How much work is the student producing? How efficient is the teacher at getting students to pass tests? We have made STEM education into a factory of sorts where young people are the product. This is not what school is supposed to be or do. School should be a place where we activate what already exists within the student. STEM is about awakening forms of brilliance that young people possess that can be used to explore, create, and connect ideas and concepts.

Schooling, sadly, has become the opposite.

To reverse this undoing, we must acknowledge the challenges to getting it done. We must return people to the interconnectedness of academic disciplines. As engineering professor YoungMoo Kim shared, "It's really, really hard to tell people who are in their boxes or in their silos, 'Hey, look around you.' When you're working on a PhD, you're supposed to become so specialized that you are the world's expert on

"In engineering and technology, every kid can turn pro."

—Lonnie Johnson, aerospace engineer and inventor of the Super Soaker your one narrow topic." The reality is, STEM preparedness is not about specialization in one topic or in one domain of knowledge. It is not about one kind of thinker or learner. It is not about any one type of gender identity or race. Rather, it is about inclusivity.

Some will say, "Yes, of course, you're right. We should be more inclusive and more interdisciplinary and interconnected." I suggest that this recognition is just the beginning. There is no reason why the tremendous imbalance in terms of gender identity, race, and socioeconomic status still exists other than the fact that STEM instruction reinforces exclusivity while it touts inclusivity. This hypocrisy—this difference between word and practice—creates a situation in which the blame is placed on those who haven't been allowed to fit within the system due to a lack of success within it. After all, if the country is pushing for STEM inclusivity, yet diverse populations are still unsuccessful, their lack of success must be their own fault. This is the current state of STEM education. The funding to support STEM participation does not match the outcomes because we lack an investment in reimagining how we define and market STEM to populations that do not fit into the existing mold of who we perceive to be smart enough to do well in it.

Technology educator Mary Beth Hertz, who is well respected for her ability to connect with young people and incorporate technology into instruction, reflected on her high school experience and said, "If someone had told me when I was in high school that girls could do this, I might actually be a developer or a programmer or in some kind of technology field outside of education. But that was just never painted as a career path for me."

All Facts, No Context

In the STEM neighborhood, expression of emotion and valuing of context are seen to be a weakness or deficiency. Such phrases as "Statistics don't lie" or "You can't argue with the numbers" are part of the unique language that reflects the culture of the neighborhood and what it attaches value to. Objectivity is placed on a pedestal as an ideal to be reached. Consequently, people hide behind it to avoid facing the way they may exclude and harm others. Objectivity is not an ideal to aspire to. Numbers without context have no true meaning and are valueless. To be objective is to be at a place of detachment from the human experience.

quantitative

It is being at a place where one is not connected to how people feel or experience the world. Objectivity does not directly equate to rigor. In fact, being emotionally connected is the first step toward deeply engaging with a phenomenon. You must care about something to unleash your passion for it—and, as many of us know, passion is the trigger for rigor.

There is a misperception that when teaching STEM subjects, there shouldn't be any cultural association with the topics. Too many teachers believe that these subjects can be taught in a vacuum. This hides the need to communicate and frame subjects in more robust and culturally engaging ways. Objectivity has been used as a shield from having to get into difficult conversations or beginning to talk about implicit bias in STEM. But what I am arguing is that there is no STEM without context. There is no rigor without invoking passion. And there is no inclusivity in thinking that does not involve diversity in who gets to fully engage and participate in STEM. Unfortunately, STEM classrooms have traditionally been deemed a place only for facts, not culture or context. This has added to the exclusionary nature of STEM and each of its associated subjects.

It is impossible to overstate the importance of highlighting contributions to STEM. Stories about people of color—in both the past and the present—who have shaped what we currently do and how we do it are essential for providing an honest and robust picture of STEM. These stories are also important so that young people from diverse backgrounds can see themselves as heroes, inventors, and participants in STEM, rather than just as consumers of it. When you do not see yourself in a subject or profession, you develop an emotional disconnect from it. For teachers with the goal to connect learners to STEM, the emotions that either exist or do not exist are essential to understand. Is there a connection and identification, or is there not? Is there a feeling of belonging, or is there not?

While rarely considered in STEM education, the emotions of the learner are a chief determinant of the type of teaching that needs to take place. There is a general misunderstanding of the ways that a particular feeling or emotion relates to how a teacher needs to introduce a subject or topic. A feeling of frustration because I do not understand how to balance an equation is very different from a feeling of anger because I dislike the science teacher or a feeling of apathy because I do not see the meaning in what is being taught. The approaches to teaching must be different based on the teacher's ability to understand the existing relationship between the student and STEM and the emotions attached to that relationship. A teacher must create space and know the particular feeling a young person has, in order to tailor the instruction to match. The educator must understand the comfort or discomfort the young person has with being able to pick up a device or microscope and then use that to connect them to the discipline.

The connecting of the young person to the disciplines is the chief responsibility of the educator. This process requires decolonizing, decontextualizing, and then recontextualizing the subjects to involve a student's unique experiences and background. Math educator Mario Benabe describes it this way: "Depending on the traditions that you draw from, you approach things differently. So, if you have students who are being embedded in a Eurocentric tradition of how they look at mathematics, they're going to judge themselves through that Eurocentric lens. In this case, what you have to do is decontextualize the existing mathematics, and then reconceptualize it in the culture and the ancestry of the person." Mario's work includes introducing Indigenous mathematics and methods for measurement and calculation that are not traditionally presented in curriculum. This approach changes the relationship of the students to mathematics and honors traditions that have been egregiously erased from learning.

Not Prepared for College—or Life

Once we start emotionally connecting young people to STEM, we must start ensuring that what we are teaching reflects what young people need to know in order to be ready for STEM-based careers. With the advent of the internet and developments in information technology, the necessary knowledge for careers in STEM or preparedness for college has shifted these last fifty years. Decades ago, young people needed to memorize a set of basic facts related to the disciplines. This basic knowledge was needed for engaging in a number of problem-solving activities that were part of working in STEM. Today, however, STEM education cannot be about memorizing information. It must be about the continued gathering, development, and application of foundational principles and conceptual understanding. I must learn how to gather the information and use it. It makes no difference if I memorize it, because I will probably end up knowing it well after using it a few times.

The reality is, all the basic facts we memorized in times past are accessible online and through a device that just about all young people always have in their possession. This is no longer an era of cramming with the goal of retaining. Today, it is more about doing. All those facts, dates, formulas, and numbers I would have crammed into my brain in the past are right there in front of me and directly accessible with a few clicks. Because of this change, a K–12 experience may offer advanced STEM classes but not actually prepare students for college courses or careers if the learning experiences in those advanced classes have sucked out all the imagination and creativity from the student.

If we want young folks in K–12 to be college and career ready, we must challenge the idea of what college and career readiness is. We also must ask, what careers are we preparing students for if they only learn to be subservient regurgitators of readily available facts? In my role as a professor, I often encounter young people who have been very successful in high school. They have taken IB and Advanced Placement courses. They then go into the science and math track and find themselves faltering, or even failing. The problem is clear: the K–12 markers of excellence do not translate into conducting research that requires content knowledge *and* creativity.

A key question we should all ask ourselves—whether educator, parent, or business owner—is the following: Do we want STEM innovators, or do we want STEM workers?

Brilliant people have been pushed from their destinies and legacies as innovators and thinkers because they have existed in conditions that fail to see them as who they are destined to be. Even when a person is technically in STEM—working for a science or technology company— they may have a STEM job, but they may not be creating, inventing, and innovating. This is unfortunate not just for people in such circumstances but for society. When this happens, we lose the opportunity to benefit from their brilliance.

 "I am, somehow, less interested in the weight and convolutions of Einstein's brain than in the near certainty that people of equal talent have lived and died in cotton fields and sweatshops." This quote from Stephen Jay Gould's book *The Panda's Thumb* captures the essence of why we must bring STEM to the people and reframe it in ways that allow them to see, find, and position themselves in these disciplines. STEM may be an arbitrary bringing together of loosely connected disciplines, but it still holds tremendous power. It is a vibrant neighborhood, with connected streets and boulevards offering great opportunity, that we want more people to have access to. How do we celebrate the beauty of the neighborhood

STEM
INSPIRATION

What It Is to Be Science-minded

Here are some skills, traits, and dispositions that engage and value science. The words shown in the cloud are what might be considered collectively as "science-mindedness."

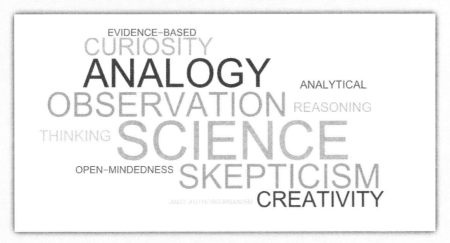

and critique its disconnection from the real world? How may we expand the neighborhood without losing its power and potential? How may we allow everyone to partake in it?

The fundamental premise of this book is to help us all break free of a tradition, a repressive framework, that does not benefit us. The overarching goal of both this book and my work is to help us see that ideas, topics, and people historically presented as separate can seamlessly and harmoniously merge. The closer we get to understanding that the silos we exist within are all self- and socially constructed, the better we can move beyond them. We need to reimagine STEM, what it means and what it embodies. The people who express the most resistance to this reimagining are indeed the people who we know need to do it the most.

This is about democratizing STEM.

This is about reengaging with it.

And this is about everybody being part of STEM and STEAM for a better world.

A sense of wonder and exploration is essential and will lead us to the key realization that the current system is not ideal. It must be dismantled, reimagined, and rebuilt. We need to be honest with ourselves, and we need to ask, *How many dreams have we crushed as a result of the way that we're currently doing things?* We must interrogate something that is so clearly broken—and sit with it. This is our responsibility as educators, as citizens of a world that values the potential of ALL students.

We were taught not to question the system. We were taught never to offer critical feedback, no matter how constructive. But we need to take an honest look at where we've been and where we are now to clearly see how we can recommit to our values and build a better world.

We are not stuck here.

STEM
TAKEAWAYS

- STEM is the merging of four subjects—science, technology, engineering, and math—that share similar elements and have numbers as a shared component. One way to think of STEM is as a neighborhood made up of streets for science, technology, and engineering, with math spoken on every corner.

- Because of deficit thinking, STEM often creates a type of trauma for students—one that many of us carry into adulthood and that changes the way we think of science and math.

- STEM education, as it exists now, is often exclusionary because it fails to recognize the importance of emotion, context, and culture. This makes it difficult for many students to identify with and find relevance in its four subjects.

- STEM still reflects past approaches to education that emphasize learning facts and numbers over developing skills such as collaboration and creativity. This means that many K–12 STEM programs fail to prepare students for college or careers.

- We can break free of this framework. To do so, we must interrogate how STEM is taught. Sit with this awareness. And begin to reimagine and rebuild how students see themselves within the context of science, technology, engineering, and math.

CHAPTER 2

Finding a Sample

I HAVE ALWAYS LOVED HIP-HOP MUSIC. Somehow, a sample from a soul record merged with a drum pattern and the poetry of a gifted rapper can strike the soul in a way that nothing else can. When I was a college student, in addition to volunteering in a science lab, working as a security guard at a medical school, and taking classes toward my STEM degree, I was a DJ at the college radio station. I took on the show at the radio station because it was an opportunity to play my favorite hip-hop songs and talk about my life—two things I needed to relieve stress. For me, the show—and, more broadly, hip-hop—was therapy. When I was on air, I could describe my work in the science lab, vent about the challenges of taking science classes while working full-time, and compare my experiences in science to my favorite hip-hop songs.

Somehow, I didn't realize that other people were listening and making connections between the life I was living and talking about and their own. People on campus would often tell me how much they enjoyed the music I played. Others would tell me how much they appreciated how honest I was about working and going to school. The most gratifying feedback came from listeners on campus who would talk to me about being a science major or even about science.

Years after graduating from college and while I attended graduate school, a friend of mine who had listened to my radio show years ago told me that the show inspired him to take science classes. He always wanted to help people and had a goal to go into the medical field, but was too intimidated by science to take any classes until he listened to my show. He mentioned that there was something about how normal the show made science seem through things I said, such as, "I gotta bounce, y'all. I gotta go back to the lab." I was a person like him, who listened to the same music and who talked about going to the science laboratory as though it was just a regular part of life. This approach made him see that he could become a biology major. There was something about the revelation of my hip-hop science identity that made him feel as though he could connect to biology.

There was a certain innovation and creativity in what I was instinctively doing. I was bringing science into storytelling and hip-hop without even thinking about it. This was before I had made my decision to be a STEM educator, a time when my goals were simply to graduate and live life. But it was also a time when I was embodying what it means to be a STEM educator. When I began teaching middle and high school science and math, I had forgotten about this story. In the classroom, I was the type of teacher who may have made my friend intimidated by science. What I was naturally doing on my radio show was showing that being a scientist is not about being stuffy or intimidating. I was activating the imagination, allowing my friend to dream beyond what he thought. To be a STEM person is to be real, relatable, and so deeply connected to the subject that it becomes a natural extension of who you are. It is to be so present that you move others to activate their imagination.

Reengage the Scientific Spirit

How do we reimagine a better future for STEM education? We do it by connecting to aspects of the discipline that align with the human desire to imagine, create, and dream. At its best, STEM is about using what we previously knew to uncover, discover, or create what we don't know or what did not exist before. It is the imagination of those in STEM that moves them to pursue the mathematical and technical knowledge that brings their vision to fruition. Whether in science, technology, engineering, or mathematics, innovation is at the heart of STEM. It is also what is needed to recruit young people to these disciplines and move them to see possibilities for their own lives that they have never seen or that they have abandoned after the world has convinced them that those possibilities are impossible.

Activist and educator Marian Wright Edelman coined the phrase, "You can't be what you can't see." These words are at the root of what drives STEM educators. We must recognize that in addition to awakening the spirit of young people, we need to show them what they can dream toward and beyond. Far too many young people are being inundated with images of themselves that are reflections of other people's perceptions of them. Their sense of self has been shaped by society, and even their dreams are manipulated by reductive images from across media.

Astronaut Leland Melvin, when talking with me about STEM and his storied career as a professional athlete and astronaut, thought back to the moon landing in 1969. Despite the impact Neil Armstrong and Buzz Aldrin had on the entire nation and our collective interest in STEM, Leland's goal was not to be an astronaut. It was to be a tennis player. He wanted to be the next Arthur Ashe. Armstrong and Aldrin were heroes that he could not see or touch. They did not look like him. They activated the imagination of the general society, but they did not do the same thing for him. Five blocks down the street from where he grew up, Arthur Ashe was practicing and learning how to play tennis. He could see Ashe winning tennis tournaments. Leland profoundly reiterated the sentiment behind Marian Wright Edelman's words: "What you see, you can be." This led me to think that if Ashe were a scientist or engineer— conducting experiments and getting recognition for his work in STEM, and if he were in close physical proximity to Leland Melvin—Leland's goals from youth would have included a passion for STEM.

Leland's story, though, becomes much more interesting precisely because he did become a STEM person. Despite not having a STEM hero in physical proximity, he found a way to dream and work into being an engineer, a football player, and an astronaut. I believe Arthur Ashe motivated Leland Melvin to dream, work hard, and pursue being a

"By making the world our classroom and our lab, we become more aware of the contours of our shared humanity."

—Satish K. Tripathil, president, University of Buffalo

professional athlete. His presence made him dream. Even though Leland did not have a professional scientist around when he was younger, there was something that caused him to dream and to subsequently develop a passion for STEM. It was in the way he was introduced to the scientist and mathematician within. At home, he was told that even though he saw himself as Arthur Ashe, there was a science and mathematics to what Arthur Ashe did. He was able to carve out an identity that included STEM and dream it into fruition because he found that STEM was all around him.

Leland remembers his mother giving him a non-OSHA-certified chemistry kit. The result? He blew up her living room. (Thankfully it wasn't major, and everyone was safe.) This was a STEM experience at home—outside the classroom. It was an experience where home life triggered some excitement. The moment he saw the explosion, his brain was activated just as was when he saw Arthur Ashe.

STEM Is All Around Us

When we teach young folks STEM, we must begin with acknowledgment of their fears and their feelings of inadequacy, brokenness, and helplessness. We begin by saying, "Don't be scared. STEM is all around you, and you're doing it all the time." Whether you are a science or mathematics educator or a technology expert, the opener is the same. For the science educator, it is, "Don't be scared. Science is all around you, and you're doing it all the time." For other educators, begin with your subject area. Then repeat the statement replacing your subject with "STEM." Young people must know that whether they are going to a park or walking down the street, every experience can be reinterpreted through the lens of science and math. They must see that it is happening all the time, in all kinds of different cultural interactions, social interactions, hobbies, and other practices that engage kids. There is STEM in all forms of art—not just highbrow museum fancy art, either. There is science and math showing up in more complex and nuanced ways in culturally rich art like graffiti. Spatial reasoning and creativity are maximized with each spray of a can to create an image that tricks the eye into thinking it is lifting off the wall. There is deep science in creating sound and a complex STEM-based knowledge needed in building and using recording studios. The work then becomes teaching young people to see STEM in the seemingly "nonscientific" facets of life. This includes finding joy in discovering the academic aspects of what is perceived to be mundane or common.

A dialogue with one of my favorite science teachers about his passion for science revealed that his STEM identity was formed during high school. It all started for him when he took an auto shop class. He took the class not because he saw any STEM-based value in it but because he was interested in cars. This class was the source of nearly all the peak moments and epiphanies he experienced in school. He remembers rebuilding an old Jeep four-cylinder engine and pouring gasoline through the carburetor. As he described it, "When it fired up, that was maybe the greatest experience I had in high school. There was nothing more satisfying than working on a car with my friends and other kids who shared my passion. Then it runs and you can drive it around a lot. That's real. That's STEM."

The experience he describes is universal. Working on something and then seeing it come to life is an experience that every child longs for and revels in. In this case, it came from working on a car—something generally perceived as blue collar. But gasoline, carburetors, engines, and the idea of internal combustion are easily connected to STEM. He was able to easily translate this experience into a career in science. I suggest that the magic is in the fact that there was a class based on something he loved. Many of us mistakenly believe that STEM happens only in labs and clean rooms. But it also happens in garages, basements, and parks. It happens in cities, on farms, and in rural areas. STEM is all around us, and nearly every topic, passion, and activity can be tied to STEM, giving it wide-ranging relevance and applicability. This must be what STEM classes acknowledge and offer—the ability to incorporate the interests of young people in a way that showcases the ubiquity of STEM and aligns with their existing passions.

Many who have read this book thus far will recognize that one of the major themes here is that educators must identify that when they are teaching young people to engage in STEM, much of what they are doing is igniting their students' passion. However, it is also important to find ways to extend that passion and excitement to families and communities. One of the fundamental arguments I make is that an underrecognized component of connecting youth to STEM is working to create environments at home and in the people whom young people love so that they can fan the flame that a teacher has sparked. It's essential, then, that any

STEM
INSPIRATION

Heritage Algorithms: Cornrow Curves

Ethnomathematician Ron Eglash has coined the term *heritage algorithms* to connect STEM with Indigenous cultures. One example is cornrows, which is a style of hair braiding. The braids have a mathematical pattern that ranges from a simple three-strand braid to a complex and layered braid pattern. These braids are an artifact that students can see and use to connect STEM to their own experiences and lives. Ron has built an online app, Cornrow Curves, where you can design your own mathematical cornrow braid. Check it out here: https://csdt.org/applications.

adults who have struggled with their STEM identity are able to see that their formative experiences may have been harmful. They must see that these experiences are not a true reflection of STEM ability. This begins by reintroducing the families and communities to the discipline, such as through materials sent home with students. The activities presented must capture the interest of the family and, ideally, tap into cultural referents to engage the recipient.

Ethnomathematician Ron Eglash, when I interviewed him for this book, talked about what he calls heritage algorithms that connect STEM with Indigenous cultures. One example is cornrows, which is a style of hair braiding in which the hair is partitioned into three sections and braided close to the scalp, usually in an underhand, upward motion. These braids are an artifact that young people can see, and the braids have a mathematical pattern to follow, ranging from a simple three-strand braid to a complex and layered braid pattern. Eglash mentions that cornrows have one foot in the past and one foot in the future and in many ways offer multiple entry points not just for young people but for families. Parents and caregivers who remember their hair being braided and who braid their children's hair feel an emotional connection to the practice. And when they are introduced to the mathematics of braiding through notes or exercises from the teacher, they can begin to see how math connects to and is ingrained in their own lives.

Anything that is culturally rich and that embodies STEM must be reintroduced to the children and to the community. A teacher may begin with recording a small video on braiding, let's say, and the math that goes into it. Then the teacher may send home a braid-based problem set with the student, or even include an invitation to parents who braid. Then, slowly, the deep mathematics in the practice gets revealed. When creating a straight cornrow style, a braider may begin with a big plat, then a smaller plat, and then an even smaller plat until the row is finished. However, if the cornrow is a curve, there are slight rotations with each plat. Eglash explains that this practice is the essence of transformational geometry. "It's scaling, rotating, and translating. The braid has done an iterative loop. The number of plats is the number of iterations. If I did a series of braids, a braid of braids, so to speak, these are my nested loops right there. You get this profound visualization of what's going on. The kinds of spirals you see are not a boring Archimedean spiral; it's this logarithmic curve. They might not know the word *logarithmic curve*, but if something clicks, when they see that, like, 'Oh, that looks cool. What if I made it curl up even tighter? How would I do that?' Well, to change the scaling factor here, immediately you dive into the fractal aspects of it."

We Are All STEM People— Even If We Don't Realize It

My point is that STEM topics exist in the hobbies, day trips, work, and vacations we all take part in. The job of educators is to reveal to the student, and then the family of the student, that there are naturally occurring enactments of STEM they are already part of. Then an effective classroom pedagogy can be built around these enactments. It also involves introducing story and history around STEM that may have been left out from much of the curriculum.

What all of us must recognize and share is that advanced scientific thinking does not require being credentialed or degreed as a scientist.

People are STEM! And they express it when they have the opportunity, environment, time, and belief (often generated externally until it triggers what already exists internally). There have been several powerful stories of folks who have careers that are not STEM related but who showcase a level of genius that confounds the establishment. Consider the story of Yu Jianchun, who, as a thirty-three-year-old delivery person, stunned the world of mathematics by finding an alternative way to make sense of Carmichael numbers—a set of large numbers that appear to be prime but are not. His accomplishment was lauded by many, including math professor Cai Tianxin, who noted, "He (Yu) has never received any systematic training in number theory nor taken advanced math classes. All he has is an instinct and an extreme sensitivity to numbers" that allowed him to develop an "imaginative solution" that hundreds of experts could not come up with.[1] The key here is that imagination does not come from formal training. It originates from passion and a perspective that operates beyond what institutions offer—*unless* institutions prioritize creating space to foster imagination.

For the educators reading this, it is important to recognize that there are pathways to activating the scientific imagination. There are practices that teachers across subject areas may enact to model the creativity and imagination inherent to STEM. This imagination and creativity require decentering established notions of who is or isn't STEM and who can or cannot do it or contribute to it. The work requires allowing ideas and concepts that are seemingly unrelated to STEM to collide in our every interaction with young people.

Among the various challenges in engaging youth in STEM, one of the most significant is that educators do not begin with the fundamental premise that STEM exists in young people. It exists in them before they enter the classroom, and it exists for them in the world beyond the classroom. Furthermore, STEM exists not only in young people but in the world among people who are not always perceived as scientists and mathematicians. Indigenous populations across the globe studied the world around them and developed complex theories centuries ago that predate contemporary scientific discovery. Some of the ideas and principles of Indigenous populations that many would consider simplistic or unscientific are often validated by STEM experts accidentally or over time.

Ron Eglash has spent a significant part of his life uncovering the hidden STEM within the cultures of those who have been pushed out of these disciplines. He spoke with me about an architect who was hired to design a building in Addis Ababa, Ethiopia. The architect, recognizing that it was important to celebrate the contributions of the Indigenous population, decided that he wanted to incorporate local African design into the new building. While researching various aesthetic approaches, he happened across an African fractal book and decided to create a fractal-based building. As he began work on the building, he began creating perforations on the building surface based on the fractals he discovered. This was an homage to the people and the context where he was building. His use of the fractals to make a design on the building (which may have been intended to be more aesthetic than functional) created amazing air flow in the building. The architect later discovered that the building was so efficient, there was no need for air conditioning, even in the building's extremely hot location. There was something in the fractal patterns beyond aesthetics. The study and use of the fractals opened a layer of complexity undiscovered until the people and their contexts were honored and studied.

The primary lesson here is that deeply engaging in STEM requires honoring the way it manifests itself in the lived experiences and histories of diverse populations.

Because effectively teaching STEM requires deeply engaging in STEM, teaching these subjects must be about honoring STEM in the students and in the contexts where they are embedded. In this way, young people might be aware of Native American treatments for malaria from the cinchona tree that predate quinine (a medicine used today to treat malaria). This is not science that came from Europe. In fact, many of the plants used to make medicine are not native to Europe at all.

When I was a seventh-grade math and science teacher, my best lessons came from honoring the STEM in my students' real lives. I remember taking students to Central Park in Manhattan and then to a local park in their neighborhood in the Bronx, New York. Without my mentioning the environment, ecology, or inequity, students naturally addressed these themes after visiting both parks. They talked about the fact that their local park looked and felt unhealthy and dirty compared to Central Park. Most important, they were able to make connections between the increase in asthma in their neighborhood, the condition of their park, and the pollution from trucks that drive through their neighborhood. As they spoke about these issues, the teaching became about working with the students to write what they observed and to explore the connections they had already made. My job as a STEM educator was to help the students see the science in the observations and connections they naturally made, and to guide them in the language of science and mathematics to articulate their organic brilliance. As a result of this experience, my students wrote letters, including detailed policy briefs to local politicians, that eventually resulted in significant changes being made to the local park. By honoring their experiences and observations, they both learned science *and* catalyzed meaningful change in their neighborhoods.

Decentering and Refocusing—a Collider Culture

Much of seeing STEM in young people's lives is about decentering whiteness. It is about expanding the notion of who and where STEM comes from by acknowledging that it has historically been exclusively male and white. The nature of how we teach must shift to center voices that have been erased from STEM, and in the centering, also prompting a collision with what's been held as traditional STEM. The goal is not an erasure of the history of STEM or those who contributed to it. Rather, the goal is an expansion of STEM through a classroom culture that welcomes collisions of thoughts, ideas, histories, and contexts.

This focus on context is not just limited to urban spaces, though. It is also essential for teaching in suburban and rural contexts. Rural settings are becoming much more diverse than ever before and often represent underresourced populations. As we emphasize the need to address inequities in STEM and through STEM, we must also consider the many places in the US where people are more than fifty miles away from a hospital or any major STEM institution. In these spaces, students rarely see doctors or scientists at work. They do not see science labs, tech incubators, or research institutions as ingrained parts of their culture. Yet STEM is all around them. It is in all they see and do, from livestock to irrigation to the stars. If they are taught to acknowledge and understand STEM in these familiar contexts, they too can begin to see themselves as participants in and drivers of science, technology, engineering, and math.

STEM educators must be comfortable embracing the conflicts that will naturally emerge when the kinds of ideas being presented here are brought into more traditional classrooms and schools. Teaching STEM in a way that sparks energy and passion in young people requires the classroom to become a collider. In particle physics, a collider is an accelerator that brings particle beams together and accelerates them to high kinetic energy so that they can impact each other. The classroom must be a collider, and the young people, the teacher, and even the curriculum are particle beams (each from different perspectives and backgrounds, requiring high energy so that they crash against each other and create something as magical as learning). Without collisions, no real learning can take place. Without conflict, there is no engagement. Therefore, it is essential for teachers to allow young people to bring their authentic selves into the classroom, to crash against curriculum and to spark learning. The greatest learning moments happen when people do not agree or when someone sees things in a new way. This is when a new perspective or a previously unconsidered truth becomes manifest.

It is in this collision—and resulting discovery and synthesis—that we have the ideal STEM classroom.

Interrogating Your Own STEM Identity

Educators need to reimagine their own identity as STEM teachers. This process is about not just academic growth but also personal growth. You need to see yourself as a project to work on. If your goal is to be a STEM educator, then view yourself as a STEM project. What books will you read? What new things will you try? What can you do to remake yourself? With ourselves, it is important that we consider the intersectionality of identity oppression and a science identity. Too often we silo ourselves, partitioning off one dimension of self because we have been told that math is hard. Or that you are not a science person. It is up to you to ask yourself, Who boxed *me* in? Reflect on who defined you so early in your life that you missed the curious, fantastic world of STEM. Who told you that you could not do it?

Often, when educators see that this identity oppression was done to them—that they experienced STEM trauma—they realize that they have been doing the same thing to others. This is when they commit to not oppressing students. Do not unintentionally reinforce the narrative of students as failures. Then you can help young folks create their own projects of self-identification, helping them be intuitive, nimble, collaborative, and reflective.

To do so, teachers must focus on science and math vocabulary, not just concepts. STEM is inaccessible to many students because they lack the language. Therefore, teaching STEM should be thought of as like teaching a foreign language. A lot of the strategies that come from folks who work on language acquisition are enormously helpful for learning STEM subjects and their accompanying language. Science, in particular, is a lived experience. Once you have the lived experience, you need the language to be able to describe the lived experience. Giving students this language will help them write themselves into the story of science. All too often, when students think of a scientist, that person is rarely someone like themselves. What does it look like to recast the story to put themselves in it?

This is the radical concept of laying claim to a scientific identity, to a scientific and STEM-based genius. A significant step toward developing this scientific identity is through "I'm a scientist" mantras that students can repeat. See the illustration of what this may look and sound like.

Do not underestimate the power of speaking yourself into a position that you didn't have before. In this way, you can help young folks understand the concept of claiming their own identity by speaking that identity into their own thoughts, their own sense of being. We need to break down these identity-based barriers and let people know what is possible when they focus on something they are passionate about. ALL students already exhibit STEM attributes. We need to look at students as whole people and honor what are traditionally seen as non-STEM attributes.

To do this, we need to reimagine what the future of STEM should look like. One key facet of this is to dig deep and integrate our humanity. Students are born with a scientific identity. We cannot separate emotions from rational thinking. If we want to go about supporting and nurturing the essence of the scientific identity, we have to understand that humans are born with it, and we cannot decouple their emotionality from their rationality. You are allowed to be human when you are doing science. We alienate way too many people who think that they cannot be scientists because they're too emotional. Or too creative. Or too artsy. Scientists, by their very nature, are creators. They are musicians, poets, and painters—they are everything.

Keep in mind, you do not have to be a great scientist to teach science, to instill that passion and curiosity in your students. No one is asking you to go back to school and be a science major. I just want you to be able to understand it, be curious enough about it, and own the fact that you can teach it. I think there is something very powerful about owning science: "I am a scientist, and I can get somebody else to be a scientist through my relationship to it." This is the articulation of educator empowerment. You do not need to be an actual scientist, technologist, engineer, or mathematician to be able to get others inspired and excited about STEM.

In the introduction to this book, I told the story of my own initiation into science through one specific class, lab, and teacher. I've heard similar stories from countless educators and education professionals across the country. If you look back on your life and you find that person who changed your life, who changed your direction, who was the catalyst for finding your passion, it is almost always a teacher. This type of teacher can be an on-ramp to a new identity that embraces STEM and the wonderment that it offers. There are entry points, and epiphanies do happen. It is not magic. It is the right teacher, the right person, the right situation. Stay open to it.

Be the teacher whom students always remember—the teacher who changed their lives.

STEM
TAKEAWAYS

- To be a STEM person is to be real, relatable, and so deeply connected to the subject that it becomes a natural extension of who you are. It is to be so present that you move others to activate their imagination.

- How do we reimagine a better future for STEM education? We do it by connecting to aspects of the discipline that align with the human desire to imagine, create, and dream. When we teach young folks STEM, we must begin with acknowledgment of their feelings of inadequacy. The work then becomes teaching young people to see STEM in the seemingly "nonscientific" facets of life, including finding joy in discovering the academic aspects of what is perceived to be common.

- STEM topics exist in hobbies, day trips, work, and vacations. The job of educators is to reveal to the student, and then the family and community of the student, that there are naturally occurring enactments of STEM that they are already a part of. It also involves introducing story and history around STEM.

- Much of seeing STEM in young people's lives is about decentering whiteness. It is about expanding the notion of where STEM comes from by acknowledging that it has historically been exclusively male and white. It is also essential to show the commonality of STEM in suburban and rural contexts.

- Teaching STEM in a way that sparks energy and passion in young people requires the classroom to become a collider. It is essential for teachers to allow young people to bring their authentic selves into the classroom, then to crash this version of self against traditionally held constructs to spark learning.

- Educators need to reimagine their own identity as STEM teachers. Do not underestimate the power of speaking yourself into a position that you didn't have before. This is also true of students—they can recast the STEM story to include themselves.

VOLUME **2**

STEAM

CHAPTER 3

CREATING A BASSLINE

H ISTORY AND CULTURE have shaped our notions of who gets to be called a scientist or a mathematician. We must be critical of these identifications, and we must introduce students to a broader understanding of what encompasses scientific and mathematical thinking.

Ethnomathematician and cybernetics professor Ron Eglash, who teaches at the University of Michigan, has spent decades studying Native Americans and their practice of bending wood. For instance, shooting a bow and arrow involves bending wood, creating tension, and storing that energy. Native American basket making is similar. The basket weaver bends pieces of wood into a very practical form of art. The same is true with wigwams, snow tubes, and canoe ribs. These all involve a series of bent, scaling sequences of curves. When Eglash asked Native American craftspeople to explain how they calculated the measurements when making a basket, they usually began by telling him how they went into the forest and dealt with the nonhumans. They then described the materials they chose in relation to their culture and history. At first, Eglash believed that the most interesting part of this wood-bending skill was the mathematical concepts it represented. But once he began to understand the process from the point of view of the Indigenous craftspeople, he realized that the basket makers believe that the wood tells them what shape it wants to be.

From a mathematical perspective, the shape Native American craftspeople create through bending wood is called a Bezier curve. A Bezier curve is defined as a parametric curve that uses polynomials as a basis. As Eglash explored this intersection of Indigenous art and mathematics, he started to wonder, who the heck was Bezier? Pierre Bezier was an engineer who worked for Renault, the French car company, in the 1950s and 1960s. Bezier "discovered" this type of geometric pattern as a means of modeling smooth curves that can be indefinitely scaled. If you went into the shop where they were designing cars, you would see a guy taking a thin piece of wood, clamping it down at both ends, and creating a curve. Bezier has now been heralded as a genius. But this is exactly what Native American craftspeople had been doing long before Bezier needed to create smooth curves for Renault's latest line of automobiles. So why does Bezier get the credit for something that has existed and been used for centuries, if not millennia?

We need to both investigate—or question—and infiltrate the STEM fields that have historically excluded certain groups of people. If we do not, then it will be much more difficult for students to understand the relevance of the skills we are trying to teach them. This process of questioning and embodying is also about repairing our dysfunctional relationships within those fields. Many of our students have formed negative impressions of math and science, believing that those subjects are only for a certain, defined group of people.

This reinforces a mistaken belief that STEM is rare, guarded, and exclusive—the realm of a certain group of people working at a specific time and in a specific place. The reality, however, is that STEM is all around us. As a part of our culture, our heritage, our ancestry, it is in all of us. This is the power of adding the *A* to STEM in order to create a fuller, more accurate, and more inclusive picture of science, technology, engineering, and math.

A Is for . . .

The *A* in STEAM is widely understood to mean art. When we think about art in the context of our classrooms, we tend to view it as a "non-academic" subject that, though important and fun, is not part of the core curriculum. This is because art is often associated with visual arts, such as painting, drawing, or sculpting. But art involves much more than drawing a picture. I argue that art *is* academic. I also argue that the *A* in STEAM refers to more than a narrow definition of art, but includes ancestry, aesthetics, and culture. It includes skills developed across centuries, often unnamed but refined to the point of expertise. In this way, we need to broaden our perspective to understand how the arts can help us to teach content better and to reinforce the development of a STEM identity.

Our narrow view of what art is and can be has prevented us from seeing the opportunities it adds to STEM learning. Yes, STEAM includes the traditional idea of art, as when students draw a cell and use different colors. But it is a lot more layered than that. The problem with a narrow view of art is that it doesn't allow us to consider the full range of possibilities for integrating the arts into our teaching. If we expand our definition, then art also encompasses an artistic worldview. Art is a holistic view of the world. An artistic worldview is one that troubles and interrogates the world and then finds what matches with internal reflection. Like artists exploring design artifacts, you start by asking questions: What does it mean? What is the significance? Why are their arms raised in a V shape? Then you begin to interpret: That means that they are reaching for something. Freedom? Hope? Opportunity? Ultimately, art is about a worldview that's critical of all phenomena.

When we think about STEAM, we must be thinking about aesthetics and not simply a drawing or painting. Aesthetics includes fields such as poetry, philosophy, music, and dance. It also includes more traditional crafts, such as basket weaving and canoe building. These can be classified into one category under aesthetic expression. Aesthetics is an appreciation for the arts, but it is also about looking at young folks as the embodiment of art. It is this idea of constructing the self as an artistic masterpiece. I allow myself to be expressed, to be created, but also to be nontraditional, to use different materials in the construction

"The culture that invigorates and enlivens today's students, hip hop, is a primary driver in helping maintain culturally relevant pedagogy's viability and usefulness."

—Gloria Ladson-Billings, educator, professor, author of *The Dreamkeepers* of myself/itself. There is something beautiful in the widening of the idea of the *A* in STEAM to include aesthetics, aesthetic forms, and aesthetic functions. The truth is, art has been colonized and can be limiting. If the acronym stands for science, technology, engineering, aesthetics, and mathematics, it is more expansive—but even still may not be expansive enough. What happens when we extend aesthetics beyond its linguistic boundaries to include the broader manifestations of human achievement?

. . . Culture?

Art is a vehicle for culture much in the same way that culture shapes art. You cannot separate the two. Recently, we've seen a big push to bring identity and culture into the classroom, but teachers may not necessarily know how to incorporate these aspects in a meaningful way. This is where the arts and aesthetics come in. You can teach STEM, as well as the arts, through a learning experience that taps into your students' culture and identity. Just think about the Native American craftspeople and their development and use of the Bezier curve—long before Bezier attached his name to it.

The STEAM classroom must do more than teach the facts and remain neutral. It has to be culturally responsive. If we do not radically shake up what STEAM is and bring into the fold people who have been categorically excluded for a long time, our efforts to improve and expand STEM education will fail. When students think of a scientist, they rarely picture themselves—at least not Black and Brown students. What if we try a different approach? If we expand our definition of art, then we can explore its application through less traditional (and more successful) models. We can validate arts education and make it more accessible by putting it into classrooms. As I mentioned earlier in the chapter, this isn't just about drawing a picture. To really integrate the arts into STEM, we must start with culture.

So what does it look like to recast this story and put ALL students in it? Art and aesthetics—the tangible, cultural dimension we can bring to STEM—offer a means of including those who have been excluded for far too long.

Changing the Narrative of Arts—and STEM

Students engage in science culture all the time; they just do not know that they are doing it because they may hold misconceptions of what STEAM looks like. Years ago, a student came into my classroom and explained how she was trying to change her friend's mind. She said that she laid out her case and included relevant and convincing examples. This student was actually engaging in the robust practices of science, but because it sounded so dissonant in relation to what people think science teaching is, she didn't realize that she was engaging in the practice.

We need to help students recognize that they already have these skills, that they are already engaging in STEM activities, and that they already embody STEM ideals.

One educator doing this work is Mario Benabe, an award-winning educator and creator of Do-the-Right-Thing-Pedagogy. He was exploring the idea of points of intersection with his students. But instead of the points being on a coordinate grid, they were on a map of Haiti and the Dominican Republic. The intersections the students identified were the borders. Mario was then able to talk about the issues that were present in Haiti and in the Dominican Republic using these points of intersection. The students who shared a cultural background with either (or both) country(ies) were interested in talking about deconstructing anti-Blackness and the social and political differences between Haiti and the Dominican Republic. Mario then did the same thing with Palestine. His students examined the issues there and explored local conflicts. They then did the same activity overlaid with their own local neighborhood in New York City. It was a way to make math real. But it was also a way to have a conversation that contextualized the concepts—points of intersection were no longer dots on a grid, but real spaces where people met, engaged in conflict, or collaborated.

The lesson? Community context and cultural nuance are too often absent from our discussions of STEM. But by bringing art, aesthetics, and culture into the conversation, we successfully add the types of contexts that create relevance. Further, one of the key artistic skills we can use to help our students bridge the divide between identity, culture, and the classroom is performance.

"Even in the most difficult times, our kids are capable of boundless joy, and their fertile imaginations provide solace when our grown-up world falls short."

—Jessica Grose, novelist and columnist for the *New York Times*

The Importance of PerformAnce

One point that many science and math teachers rarely consider is that the communication of STEM is an art form. You may have the best hypothesis or the most intricate equipment, but if you have a boring presentation and are unskilled at narrative, no one will listen to your idea. Not only is there an art to the pedagogy of a teacher; there is also an art to being able to communicate ideas. This is especially important now, as STEM literacy is becoming a vital part of societal practice. The ability to engage in a robust discussion, debate ideas, and persuade people is essential. You can do all the research you want, but if you do not know how to convince people, your ideas will go nowhere.

Stephanie, one of my graduate students, was a competitive figure skater for eight years and an actor for twelve years. She explained that before pursuing STEM, her life had been centered around performance. She remembers how, during her first skating competition, she was so nervous that her routine was a disaster. During her first play in fifth grade, another character talked over her only speaking line, ruining her performance. These sound like small bumps, but looking back, Stephanie realized that these performances taught her how to act under pressure, be confident, and handle disappointment, as well as use other social skills—making friends, expressing herself, and daring to be different.

This ability to perform is especially important today with our "attention economy." The people, products, and innovations that do best and gain traction are the ones that get the most attention. Marketing scientific knowledge has to be done through an artistic forum. The art of performance extends to modern success skills as well. One of the biggest complaints that companies have about young people who come into the workforce is that they lack proficiency in the key skill of speaking up in a meeting. The young people are thus limiting themselves and their ability to have an impact. This is problematic for many reasons, but the good news is that the tools to correct the issue are readily available to us.

Hip-hop is one of those tools. A hip-hop artist is a person who can stand on stage and command an audience, the same way a teacher can command their audience of learners. With hip-hop, you can teach students how to learn words and their meanings so that they can expand their vocabulary. Once they have created raps, students then should annotate the lyrics. The Common Core learning standards have kids

GZA—Rapper, "Spiritual Head," and Science Advocate

GZA, or Gary Earl Grice, is a founding member of the seminal hip-hop group the Wu-Tang Clan, as well as a successful solo artist. His solo album *Liquid Swords* reached platinum status and was lauded for its complex lyricism and hypnotic style. GZA is more than a world-renowned musician, though. He's also a powerful advocate for science and math education. Search online using the keywords "TEDxTeen GZA" to hear his talk on the genius of science.

Check it out. The video also includes two student Science Genius performers, Victoria Richardson (profiled in this book), and Jarbari Johnson, a competition-winning artist for his rap "Quest for Joulelry."

To read more about the Science Genius event, visit hiphoped.com/science-genius.

memorizing, reading, and writing nonfiction texts. If they write in a rhyme, they are writing a nonfiction text. You want kids to be metacognitive—thinking about what they are thinking. If they are performing their rhyme and rewriting and rethinking their rhymes, they're engaging in deep and complex metacognition. In this way, engaging in a hip-hop-based pedagogical practice actually surpasses the expectations of the existing standards for education.

An Intersection of Disciplines

Incorporating the arts is not as difficult as it may seem. It could be as simple as asking students to physically act out math problems, demonstrate scientific experiments and principles, reenact historical events, or perform scenes from literature. There is value in understanding that art has meaning beyond the product. For example, a class I recently observed had an art component that asked students to construct blueprints for the ant farm they were building. It is an inquiry project in which students observe how ant colonies operate. The intent of the project was to show students the concrete connections between science and art. Engineers need to know how to imagine, create, and draw. This type of project enables students to learn the skills essential for academic growth, while also letting them practice so-called soft skills, such as collaboration and creativity.

This is a critical intersection of disciplines. Recently, I did an interview at the Lincoln Center for the Performing Arts focused on the arts and arts education. The people I spoke to are grappling with the same issues we see in STEM classrooms: they want more interest in and validation for the arts. The arts education community is pushing toward standardization and professionalization. For this reason, the arts are following the scientific model for the sake of validation. This is a fascinating conundrum: while science needs to move more toward the arts, the arts are trying to move toward science. Everybody is chasing each other—and no one is getting anywhere.

But this much is clear: STEM is creative, though many of us may not see it that way. To get anywhere, we all need to think outside the box. What if we tried this? What if we incorporated this aesthetic principle or that cultural artifact? This is how we can move further. I have always understood STEM this way—as a very creative endeavor. As I learned while talking with artists at Lincoln Center, science and art are not so different from each other. Both are responses to cultural and historical moments. We create art or pursue scientific inquiry as a means of processing our world. They both represent a very human response: to create meaning out of the information we gather, to learn from it, and to progress. Because of this similarity, forming a STEM identity is about examining our ancestries in a way that gives us permission to be a scientist, to be a mathematician, and to be an artist.

Before we move on, I want to leave you with one more example of the power of the *A* in STEAM. For a semester, students paid close attention to how their teachers approached student engagement. As a final presentation, the students put on a play in which they reenacted all of the times teachers alienated them in the classroom when they attempted to engage. The performance was nothing short of earth shaking. Students took this enormous volume of qualitative and quantitative research, crystallized it, and enacted it. They could have presented it as a poster, but a poster would not shift my opinion as much as this half-hour ensemble performance. These brilliant high schoolers all across New York sat in classrooms and gathered literally hours and hours of data and then presented it through art. My point is that art is not only essential—it is the final manifestation of how we disseminate STEAM knowledge.

STEAM
TAKEAWAYS

- The reality is that STEM is all around us. As a part of our culture, our heritage, our ancestry, it is in all of us. This is the power of adding the *A* to STEM in order to create a fuller, more accurate, and more inclusive picture of science, technology, engineering, and math.

- The *A* in STEAM is widely understood to mean art. But the *A* in STEAM refers to more than a narrow definition of art. It includes ancestry, aesthetics, and culture. We need to broaden our perspective to understand how the arts can help reinforce the development of a STEM identity.

- The STEAM classroom must do more than teach the facts and remain neutral. It has to be culturally responsive. If we do not radically shake up what STEAM is and bring into the fold people who have been categorically excluded for a long time, our efforts to improve and expand STEM education will fail.

- We need to help students recognize that they already have these skills, that they are already engaging in STEM activities and already embody STEM ideals. By bringing art, aesthetics, and culture into the conversation, we are able to add the types of contexts that create relevance.

- Science and art are both responses to cultural and historical moments. We create art or pursue scientific inquiry as a means of processing our world. They both represent a very human response: to create meaning out of the information we gather, to learn from it, and to progress.

CHAPTER 4

ADDING THE DRUMBEAT

FOR FIFTEEN YEARS, Jeffrey Henderson worked as a footwear designer for Nike—a dream job for many people of all ages and backgrounds. He then founded an award-winning design firm named AndThem, which has collaborated with sneaker and apparel companies such as Yeezy, Allbirds, Koio, Converse, and Everlane. Even with this incredible background as a designer and businessman, Jeffrey believes that he is, first and foremost, a problem solver. In this overarching capacity, he combines a STEM background with STEAM-based skills, such as drawing and drafting, presenting (performance), organizational communication, and collaboration. One of the questions he often asks himself is: How do you create something from nothing? This combination of skills has enabled Jeffrey to approach his work systematically, but also with a deep appreciation and understanding of beauty. Take a look on Instagram (@jeffreyalanhenderson) and you can find amazing

STEAM
INSPIRATION

Jeffrey Henderson—Shoe Blueprint

The perfect alchemy of science and art, of STEM and STEAM, is clearly illustrated in this blueprint of a shoe.

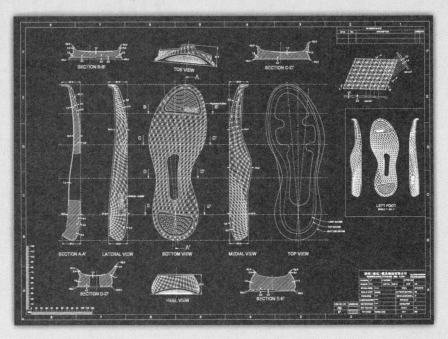

images of his work—work that offers a perfect illustration of the confluence of technology and design, of science and aesthetics. Jeffrey excels in a space where STEM and STEAM come together. His understanding of science and math, of materials and geometry, takes shape through an understanding of aesthetics and culture. Without this alchemy, it is just rubber and nylon that covers your foot, rather than a social icon that inspires people to the point of obsession.

The arts offer STEM a human grounding. In this way, the arts contribute to discoveries and innovations that change the way we understand and interact with our world. By examining the humanistic qualities of those who engage in STEM, we can recognize how art and science have the greatest potential when working together. There is an old saying, "No root, no fruit." With art, aesthetics, and culture, it is the same. They are the root that helps STEM blossom and provide the fruit, the innovations we all have come to expect from medicine and technology. They are also the root that helps students find relevance in STEM by connecting science, technology, engineering, and math to their own experiences and lives.

The Root—A Human Grounding

Science is theoretical. And once you get past addition, subtraction, multiplication, and division, math becomes very theoretical. We could disagree on semantics, but this is how most people think of these topics. To move from theory to application, we need to make STEM more approachable, understandable, and relevant to our students by incorporating the arts. How we go about doing this will be influenced by the different cultures, backgrounds, and knowledge bases that we encounter in the classroom. As I discussed in the previous chapter, helping students see the connections between their culture and the culture of STEM will make it more approachable. Our students are more likely to engage with science if we begin with something they know.

Science is, in essence, a quest to understand the world, to reveal the secrets of creation and continued life. Art has that same drive. But art, aesthetics, and culture are not bound by the same rigid rules as many STEM subjects. With art, students are freer to explore possibilities. The arts offer boundless opportunities to make sense of the world. If we weave together these different forms, we facilitate both learning and innovating, both absorbing and applying.

The scientific process involves converting data to information and then turning information into knowledge. But the language of science isn't always accessible to everyone. Art can be a means of expression that helps communicate the data that science creates. Many people who work with very large data sets know this to be true. This is why data visualization—the turning of raw data into easily digested graphics, charts, and diagrams—is such a vital component of data analytics. There is a clear connection between the language of art and the language of science. And, in truth, there is no way to separate the two: science informs art, and art informs science. Together, they help explore and explain the world around us.

Kenric Allado-McDowell is head of Google's Artists and Machine Intelligence program (AMI). Through this unique role, Kenric can bring artists, philosophers, and critics directly into engagement with the artificial intelligence (AI) technologists at Google. These artists work with the most cutting-edge technology and are able to ask questions such as, "Did you think about nonhumans as actors? Did you think about radical forms like architecture? How is your AI system going to accommodate the landscape?" In this way, artists inform science through the addition of human imagination and humanistic concerns. In addition, innovative artists can take advantage of Google's AI technology to help create new, innovative art. In this way, it is a two-way street that opens opportunity to both artists and scientists, imagineers and engineers.

People in STEM have yet to recognize that art is a professional field with its own criteria. They argue that making art is simple and subjective; what qualifies as good art is up to the viewer. But this is not true. Art, philosophy, literature, graphics, painting—they all have their own criteria, their own language, their own aesthetic. Much like scientific discoveries, they must show a degree of relevance and survive years of review and criticism. They all have their own boundaries, their own expectations. These criteria are what add to, and often underpin, the science and the technology.

The Fruit—Creativity, Innovation

If we think about the most brilliant, most prolific, most iconic scientists of our time, what attributes do they display? First, folks think about the Albert Einsteins of the world. So, what makes Einstein Einstein? It was not that he was a genius at memorization. Einstein was creative. He was imaginative. He spoke in metaphor and analogy. His quotes that relate to music and philosophy are better known and more popular than his quotes that relate to science. He was inquisitive. He was antiauthoritarian. He described information in unique ways.

He engaged in improvisation.

A Lingua Franca

Improvisation, as practiced in jazz, is the process of innovating—of trying new techniques and new combinations—in the hope of creating

"Creativity is the history of science and innovation."

—Chris Emdin

something better. But in many cases, these attempts fail. Improvisation is a big part of the creative process. With improvisation comes risk-taking and a confidence and versatility such that even if you make a mistake, you can find the right way. Music brings to science the practice of improvisation and the acceptance of failure, to innovate, create, dream, build, grow, and evolve.

Stephon Alexander, a physicist and jazz musician, grew up in the Bronx, which many argue is the birthplace of hip-hop. He believes that the particular conditions in the Bronx—the coexistence of different groups of people from different cultural backgrounds—were a catalyst for many of the innovations in hip-hop music and hip-hop culture. For most of Alexander's academic training as a physicist, he integrated music and science. Once he started seeing the elements of this integration in his research, he began to look at his work in a completely different way. For him, incorporating some of the practices of hip-hop and jazz music has been essential for his work in physics. New innovations and new ideas enhanced his research.

Music truly is the lingua franca—the common language—of humankind. It is the one language everybody speaks. So, when students walk into the classroom and they hear an instrumental that they can hear outside the classroom, there's a blurring of the divide between the in-school and out-of-school worlds. And hip-hop is the voice of the youth. It has been since its inception. It is easy to bridge the gap between hip-hop and the classroom because many kids listen to hip-hop. What I have been doing through Science Genius and through Urban Science Education is replicating the teaching and learning spaces already in hip-hop and then bringing them into the traditional classroom. What we are doing is saying, "Let the kids be able to describe the scientific ideas conceptually, using their own localized language, using their own means of talking." It is the notion that you can use your own words to describe scientific ideas and that there is a safe space to do it, one that values inclusion and acceptance.

What does this look like in the classroom? GZA (one of the founding members of the Wu-Tang Clan) provides a model for students to explain their scientific concepts through recitation and rhymes. He shows them how to structure a rhyme, what words to use, where to put them, and how to make the story compelling and descriptive. First, he teaches them to make the rhyme "half short, twice strong," encouraging students to be as visual as possible and really put time and thought into their language.

For instance, he might give the example of a rhyme about dark matter, using words such as *light* and *bright*. He will point out that these are simple words and that a lot of emcees use them. Creating a good rhyme is about taking the words and making a sentence structure as strong as possible. So GZA might start his rhyme by saying, "Before space and time, thought produced a speck of light. It was infinitely hot and so extremely bright." It's about showing the students how to structure a convincing rhyme and making it as tight as possible.

And, of course, there is the age-old hip-hop art of competition. Students know that they are in competition with kids in other spaces, so they must make sure that their rhymes are good enough to be able to withstand a rigorous battle. This motivates them to work on their rhymes and prepare themselves to perform like an emcee.

The characteristics of the most brilliant and prolific scientists of our time—whether it's Einstein or Marie Curie or Niels Bohr—are also found in hip-hop emcees. Every emcee thinks in metaphor and analogy and is a skeptic. Emcees also exhibit the idea of "keepin' it 100" (authentic and truthful). Their practice is antiauthoritarian and evidence based. You cannot make a claim in the world of science without it being backed up by others who are also within your discipline. Likewise, you cannot make a claim within hip-hop about how strong your rhymes are without the backing of others. You have to keep it real. You have to keep it 100. If our students are inherently emcees, STEAM can, in addition to teaching the content, expose them to all the skills, traits, and dispositions of the most prolific and brilliant scientists of our time.

There Is an App for That

Marcus Blackwell, CEO and founder of Make Music Count, has created an app that helps students improve their math skills by playing popular songs on the piano. The great thing about the app is that you do not need to know how to play the piano to get started. Blackwell and his team took everything that had a musical definition and gave it a math definition, looking at the piano as if it were a number line. When you add numbers, you move to the right on the keys. When you subtract numbers, you move to the left. The answers to the math questions are the notes needed to play the song on the piano. When you finish a section, your reward is music. The answers light up, and you play the notes as they light up. Again, those notes were the notes you solved for in the math equations.

STEAM INSPIRATION

Neil deGrasse Tyson—Counterpoint

"I think STEAM is misguided in the following sense. The art world saw that STEM was a really cool acronym and that it was stimulating people to give money. It's my opinion that the arts community wanted to piggyback on the science community for funding because arts are always underfunded. They invented a premise that I think is false. The premise is that the scientist needs art in order to be a creative scientist. And there's no real evidence for that. Yes, you have to be creative to be a scientist. But there's no real evidence that formal training in the arts is the source of that creativity. What is true, however, is that science influences art. It's not a two-way street. It's nine tenths one way, and one tenth the other way. Because for example, when scientists invent a new material, artists are all over it. Good artists track the discoveries of science and innovate through those discoveries. But you cannot declare that scientists on the frontier innovate by reaching to art."

When students finish a lesson, they must also complete a math quiz without music. This is how Marcus strengthened the focus on math. He wanted to make sure that students understand that the key takeaway is not that you can play Migos; it is that you showed your understanding of how to add and subtract fractions and whole numbers on a piano. In his app, you will find everything from Migos to Taylor Swift to the Jetsons. Through this platform, Marcus has created a means of embedding the discourse around mathematics in what kids do every day. As a result, the app shows students that they are capable of doing the math—they just need the right incentive.

Our Multidimensional Nature

Why is it that a student cannot memorize multiplication tables, but can memorize dozens of raps, rhymes, and songs? It has taken us far too long to recognize that there is a difference between rigorous knowledge and mere regurgitation. Memorization drills do not work. What does work are activities that engage students emotionally and connect to what they already know. This is where the *A* in STEAM sparkles. Teaching STEM concepts using the arts not only connects to students' lives but also taps into their existing identities. And in doing so, it extends that identity to include a STEM identity.

The division of disciplines ends up hurting people. If we truly examine all the separate disciplines, they share many of the same skills. It is not that you are a math or history or English person; every one of those specialties uses critical thinking. Everybody needs to collaborate. Everybody needs to be creative. My biology advisor when I was an undergraduate told me, "If you want to be a biologist, you need to be an English major. You need to be a statistician. You need to be a historian." She explained to me that I needed to embrace these different subjects to understand how "life," the subject of biology, truly works. We try to teach certain skill sets to our students, but there are many ways to approach a subject or create the type of relevance that supports rigor. We need to be sure to include the arts as we think about student motivation and the ways that students may plug into an activity.

Several years ago, I attended an "Influencers Dinner" at Columbia. The guest list included noted scientists, businesspeople, politicians, and other community members. Over the course of the evening, we all had to guess what everyone else did, without giving away our own profession. As you can imagine, everybody missed the mark—by a lot. Then we had to share what we wanted to do with our lives. One of the attendees, Dr. Joachim Frank, a Nobel Prize–winning chemist, admitted that his dream is to be a fiction writer. Intrigued, I asked him to tell me more about his interest in fiction. His imagination and creativity, he said, have been developed through his fiction. By exploring literature, writing, and art, he has created a form of "peripheral vision"—an ability to look toward the edges and fringes—that informs his scientific research. When an experiment does not work or a hypothesis fails, he looks to the more humanistic pursuits in his life for inspiration. As he explained, the big, Nobel Prize–level breakthroughs happen because something unexpected influences his thinking.

We need to look at scientists as whole people who can tap into these nontraditional domains. Similarly, we need to step back and look at the humanity of the children in front of us. How do we honor the non-STEM attributes of young folks and use those as starting points for joining the STEM-STEAM world? This humanistic consideration is what will transfer to the next year, the next classroom, and to a future career. If we support young people as they examine, think critically, and form a human connection to the material, they are far more likely to remember it. We remember what we feel.

We need to teach from this STEAM-based point of view.

STEAM
TAKEAWAYS

- The arts offer STEM a human grounding and help students connect to the content. By looking at our students as whole people, we can tap into their non-STEM attributes as an entry point for their journey into the STEM-STEAM world.

- The arts can help make STEM more accessible. Traditionally, science has been seen as theoretical and difficult to understand. But artistic fields help us explore and explain our world. To effectively communicate STEM ideas, we need to utilize more humanistic skills.

- Skills cultivated by the arts—such as creativity, innovation, and improvisation—contribute to new discoveries that can change our world.

- Relevant content connects to students' lives. The arts help form that connection by accessing students' existing knowledge and skills. Using hip-hop to teach students about dark matter, for example, gives them an immediate entry point into the material, even if they're unfamiliar with the vocabulary.

- A division of disciplines does not serve STEM or our students. Rather, we should emphasize how having an artistic background may build on and enhance academic knowledge in STEM fields.

CHAPTER 5

DROPPING THE SPRINKLES

E MBRACING YOUR STEAM IDENTITY and becoming a STEAM educator take courage. But you cannot build courage in young people without putting a little work into yourself first. As teachers, we need to utilize STEAM affirmations. Try writing down a list of positive affirmations—for example, "I do not need to get all the answers right." These are things you can say to yourself to help reimagine the STEM and STEAM disciplines. Then you can have your students repeat these back to themselves. This is part of the STEAM identity formation between the teacher and the students.

When I think about my own STEAM identity, I know I am a work in progress. I know I am a project. In a sense, we are all projects. If your goal is to be a STEAM educator, then view yourself as a STEAM project. What will you read? What will you try? How will you experiment? What can you do that allows you to reimagine yourself? Think of your own personal STEAM project as the process of becoming a STEAM educator. And then, by modeling this, you can help young folks create their own projects, including reimagining a STEM-STEAM identity.

The STEAM subjects are about being flexible. Likewise, the pedagogy and the framing must consider how to make this more comfortable for all teachers, as well as students. Recently, one of my favorite words has been *nimble*. In this day and age, being nimble—at work, at home, with oneself—is a superlative skill. One way to become nimbler is by collaborating with other educators.

Advocate for Collaboration

As educators, we often focus on collaboration among students, but not among ourselves. This is a mistake. In a perfect world, the math teacher and the art teacher plan together. When I was in the classroom, we teachers had inside jokes. We would laugh together, share notes, and plan together. If the history teacher was talking about industrialization, I was working with my class on how peppered moths adapted during industrialization and evolved through natural selection. There was this holistic connection between our content because we were keeping our doors open and talking to each other.

Teachers need to advocate for spaces where they can interact with one another across disciplines. The system, as it exists, has people teaching inside silos. Science, technology, engineering, and math teachers need to start reimagining how they look at themselves. Our thinking must not be that we teach just one subject. Instead, our presence needs to be as a STEAM teacher. This is a piece of the discourse that rarely exists. There are practical things that you can do as you construct an identity as a STEAM educator. Think about a few simple questions: When you introduce yourself to the class, how do you present yourself? How do you center art in your math instruction? How do you include engineering when you are teaching science principles? This is something tangible for practitioners in each of the domains.

For some schools, such as the Science Leadership Academy in Philadelphia, planning is almost always interdisciplinary. Within the school culture, there's the understanding that math and art are best combined, and this type of combination occurs across the subjects. Teachers are encouraged to design their course work. To help, teachers have the space during staff meetings for interdisciplinary conversations that will then impact their lesson planning.

For the science and math teachers reading this book, it is essential that you advocate for yourself by articulating to the administration the need for intentional, interdisciplinary planning time. When it comes to scheduling for the academic year, it is critical to emphasize the significance of having science, math, and art teachers in the same space.

Similarly, give students the opportunity to collaborate with one another and with the teacher. Students may be empowered to design their own lessons. Help the students understand some basic points and then consider letting the students teach the lesson. You can write down what you learned about how your students engage with one another and what examples you can use in your next lesson. The following are some other ways to bring STEAM into your classroom:

- Forge connections with the scientific and artistic community outside the classroom building.
- Research science and art folks in the world.
- Reach out to somebody at your local college or university.
- Identify a musician outside the school building who has a fascinating story you can share with young people.

These are all relatively easy ways to offer more interdisciplinary opportunities to your students. Another way to create a STEAM culture in your classroom is through project based learning.

The Power of Projects and Presentation

Project based learning, or PBL, offers an academic way to incorporate STEAM in the classroom. It is a pedagogical platform for which teachers can easily find activities and lesson plans. STEAM and PBL go hand in hand, especially if you are trying to approach learning in a culturally responsive way.

When I was in the classroom, I made sure that students knew they needed to learn how to build things to do STEAM. In one of my botany classes, kids did a greenscaping project around the school. They acted as landscape architects, and the teachers were their clients. They interviewed their teachers to ask them, How would you like to make your room greener? The teachers shared what they wanted in their room, and the kids designed blueprints. Then the teacher gave them feedback on whether they liked the designs or not, and the students built the chosen design. This project brought together science skills, math skills, art skills, and collaborative skills. In this way, it was a true STEAM experience.

I spoke with Bob Lenz, CEO of PBLWorks, a company that provides tools and research to help teachers design and implement quality PBL. Bob said that when he was running schools, PBL is how they got kids excited about science, math, and technology. For instance, they did a physics project that required kids to create model cars, as for a soapbox derby. They had to use physics to make projections of how fast the car would go. At the end, they had a competition, and they videotaped the cars going down the stairwell at the school. A team watched the video and calculated the speed of the cars. Then they presented all of this to an audience in real time.

As you can likely see from the previous examples, PBL enables students to demonstrate and apply their knowledge in real-world settings. Students engage in workplace learning experiences in STEM fields by doing actual projects and working with real people. This is especially beneficial for students of color. Students see not only how the learning is applied but also that there are people with similar backgrounds and cultural experiences doing this work. This helps with the development of a STEM-STEAM identity. If you are interested in implementing PBL in your own classroom, see the Essential Project Design Elements Checklist from PBLWorks, found in the appendix.

Performance—in the form of a public presentation—is a critical component of any quality PBL experience. Because they have an authentic audience, learners will work more diligently and accept the challenge in a way that is completely different from how they approach a normal classroom assignment. It is a natural process. If you know that you are required to present your ideas in public, you will work harder because you do not want to be embarrassed. This also makes the project's result more relevant and authentic, with students gaining a sense of working toward mastery. It is not just another assignment students are completing; they are trying to become an expert in that field.

This type of public performance is part of a valuable metacognitive experience. Students need to reflect on what they will say and how they will say it. This reflection is part of a transformative experience in which students learn something about themselves. As we educators are trying to get more kids interested in STEM-STEAM, these are the types of peak experiences that make students say, *Whoa, I can do this. I'm actually good at this. I enjoyed it. I want to learn more about this.* If you just did a project and didn't share it publicly, it goes in a file or in the trash can. The public performance gives it a sense of purpose. None of us do work just to do work. PBL draws on the same idea in school, giving learners a clear goal and true audience. In this way, the public performance element of PBL increases the relevance of the project.

When you offer PBL in a systematic way, students have an opportunity to present multiple times. As with anything in life, the more they do it, the better and more confident they get. At the Envision Schools, which Bob Lenz founded, public presentations were a regular part of the curriculum. As Bob told me, once these Envision students went to college and had to do a presentation their freshman year, they were surprised to learn that their college classmates were terrified of public speaking. It was similar with skills such as collaboration and teamwork. Too often, and in too many schools, students aren't given opportunities to develop their teamwork skills. They are used to working alone while taking tests or writing papers. But then they get into college courses that require group work and may lack an understanding of the roles and goals that drive good collaboration. Students who have experienced PBL, however, know how to act as facilitators or note takers. Because they have this skill base, they have a sense of efficacy and agency.

Problem solving, presenting, and collaborating—these are truly future success skills in all fields, but especially in STEM-based careers.

The *T* in STEAM

Another way STEAM can provide essential success skills for the future is through the integration of technology, especially through music and digital arts programs. An example of this is hip-hop curriculum. Having to write a song is rigorous. Then, having to produce it involves technology. After producing the song, students need to perform it, which ties back to the importance and utility of performance.

Similarly, you can integrate technology using a blending of performing arts. For instance, Bob Lenz described a PBL art piece called American Voices. There are different versions of this project, but the core idea is that students conduct interviews with real people. In one version, students interview recent immigrants, sometimes even people in their

"The arts and sciences
are avatars of
human creativity."

—Mae Jemison, engineer, physician,
and former NASA astronaut

STEAM
INSPIRATION

When Artists and Scientists Collaborate

Janani Balasubramanian is an artist and researcher working at the intersections of art and science. Janani's work is rooted in collaborations with scientists, through which they discover how artistic inquiry can meet, expand, and provoke new thought in relation to a given scientific discipline. In collaborating with scientists from myriad fields, Janani has found that their involvement prompts an emotional depth that doesn't usually exist. One of their overarching goals with this collaboration is to "take back physics, math, and other disciplines to become spaces that are full of love and softness, as well as rigor." They say, "I give the scientists a dose of humanity that is frequently lost in the pursuance of scientific work." Find out more about Janani and their work here: https://jananibalasubramanian.com/.

own family. From the interviews, they create public radio–type, short audio documentaries. They then create websites that include citations and references for their research. Or students take their interviews and create a monologue. Then they can perform this monologue in front of a digital backdrop of photographs and art. Through this type of merging of arts and technology, students learn about research and data collection, as well as how to use digital technology tools and processes. They learn communication and presentation skills and how to synthesize varied ideas.

Social media—Instagram, TikTok, Twitter, and the like—offers platforms for experimenting with and sharing art. These forms of self-expression can help contribute to a STEM-STEAM identity. David Sikabwe, a University of Texas at Austin computer science student, became a Twitter sensation with his remix of the Frank Sinatra classic "Fly Me to the Moon." Sikabwe pulled from all aspects of his education to write the song lyrics, adding an original verse that features scientific wordplay. As a computer science major, David said he is essentially majoring in problem solving, and this carries over into his song writing: "With songwriting, you've got something you want to say, a goal, and you want to find the

STEAM
INSPIRATION

Google Deep Dream Generator

The Deep Dream Generator is part of Google's Human Artificial Intelligence Collaboration. It is a computer vision program that was initially designed to help scientists and engineers understand what a deep neural network is seeing when it looks at a given image. The program uses what is called a "convolutional neural network" to enhance patterns through an algorithm that creates a dream-like hallucinogenic appearance. The platform is free and can be found at deepdreamgenerator.com.

Before

After

most efficient and effective way to say it." His well-crafted remix even got him noticed by *Hamilton* creator Lin-Manuel Miranda. To see David's work, take a look at his Twitter account: @thustweetsdavid.

Technology as the Artist

In the previous chapter, we met Kenric Allado-McDowell, the head of Google Artists and Machine Intelligence (AMI). As part of Google AMI, Kenric and his team have developed a tool called the Deep Dream Generator. Artists have always searched for new tools to enhance their work, from adding new paint colors or new materials to adopting new technologies. Google's Deep Dream project taps into this impulse and helps connect artists with AI to create original images. The Deep Dream Generator uses artificial neural networks that learn from large sets of example data, rather than human operators. These networks are typically used to classify images and recognize objects within those images. By feeding the networks a variety of examples, the AI algorithms can start to pick out different features. Then, once the networks are trained, they can also be used to create new imagery. An example input and output from the Deep Dream Generator is included here.

Here is how this Deep Dream Generator works: the network is shown an initial image and begins to classify and interpret it. Then the user decides what elements the software should focus on, altering the image to modify its content. These steps are repeated until a new picture appears. The results can vary from simple geometric patterns to psychedelic-looking pieces that resemble a Salvador Dalí painting. Google has tested this program with well-known artists who created pieces that were then sold at a charity event. "Whether it's a new paintbrush or pigment or neural network, they are all potentially great tools for creating sophisticated art," said Christiane Paul, the adjunct curator of new media arts at the Whitney Museum of American Art. In this way, technology can—and should—be seen as a tool for creation instead of just a tool for consumption.

STEAM
TAKEAWAYS

- If your goal is to be a STEAM educator, then you need to view yourself as a STEAM project. Think about the types of professional development that will help build this identity and support your work in the classroom. By modeling this growth, you can also help students create their own STEAM identities.

- Teachers need to advocate for spaces where they can collaborate with other teachers. This kind of interdisciplinary planning and communication not only helps students see the overlap among disciplines but also helps them connect the content to real-world applications.

- Project based learning offers an approachable academic platform for incorporating STEAM in the classroom. PBL helps get students excited about STEM, enables them to demonstrate and apply their knowledge, increases relevance, and teaches twenty-first-century success skills.

- You can bring STEAM into your classroom through the integration of technology. Technology has become an artistic platform, which allows for a more seamless blending of the two worlds through music and arts programs at school.

VOLUME 3

MAKE

CHAPTER 6

LAYING OUT THE SONG STEPS

THE *MAKER MOVEMENT* is the umbrella term for independent inventors, designers, and tinkerers. A convergence of computer hackers and traditional artisans, the niche is established enough to have its own magazine, *Make*, as well as hands-on Maker Faires that attract DIYers from across the country and around the world. Makers tap into an American admiration for self-reliance and combine that with open-source learning, contemporary design, and powerful personal technology, such as 3-D printers. The creations, born in cluttered local workshops, garages, and bedroom offices, stir the imaginations of consumers numbed by generic, mass-produced, made-in-China merchandise.

Although the maker movement's roots are tech related, there are often people at maker shows teaching crochet, jewelry making, and even how to pickle vegetables and make jams and jellies. The movement has the potential to bring techies and nontechies alike into the world of being creators; some are hobby related, but many end up making great products and selling them online. Websites such as Etsy and eBay have become powerful vehicles for makers to sell their wares to users around the world.

Part of why making has become so popular is because of the growing accessibility of technology and materials. The costs for tools such as 3-D printers, CNC mills, and Arduino and Raspberry PI motherboards are in reach of normal consumers. Resources such as *Make* magazine (makezine.com), books, podcasts, and YouTube videos for do-it-yourselfers have grown exponentially and are getting more and more people interested in being makers of some sort.

Making transcends traditional boundaries of vocation or area of study. There is an inherent freedom in making that has unbridled potential to tap into a person's creativity. Max Lawrence, cofounder of Space1026, explains it well: "You should be able to go into a place and be like, I would like to express myself through 3D. I would like to express myself through computer programming. I would like to express myself through wood. I'd like to build this thing, be able to have a focused end goal, and to explore all the possibilities inside of that." Because it is inherently interdisciplinary, making develops multiple competencies and frees a student from having to choose one interest.

It is essential that we teach kids to believe in themselves, to believe that they can imagine, create, and navigate adversities. This means that as teachers, we need to let go of a certain amount of control so that students can take thoughtful risks and learn to revise their pathways to achieve their goals. At the same time, we must also facilitate learning in a way that is not overwhelming to the point of disengagement. Making helps accomplish both goals.

A Brief History of Making

Most people think of making as the application of the engineering concepts in STEAM, but it is actually the amalgamation of all aspects of science, technology, engineering, art, and mathematics. The modern maker movement began in the 1980s, stemming from the theory of constructionism by Seymour Papert, which builds on Piaget's ideas of cognitive development.[1] According to these theories, humans learn most

"The maker movement has the opportunity to transform education by inviting students to be something other than consumers of education. They can become makers and creators of their own educational lives, moving from being directed to do something to becoming self-directed, independent learners."

—Dale Dougherty, president, Make Community, founder of *Make* magazine and Maker Faire effectively when they have the opportunity to create, tinker, make, and build.

Makerspaces embody this theory through the application of STEAM to bring a maker's ideas to life.

The original maker movement began in the tech world where inventors, designers, and tinkerers began to congregate to play with materials, create, and eventually start solving problems or creating products to sell.[2] At Maker Faires, these creatives showcase their talents and build a community. The maker culture began as an empowering endeavor in which people figured out how to increase self-efficacy through DIY projects for repair, modification, or enhancing their own environment. This culture exploded into a global phenomenon with people creating makerspaces to work together and control their own means of production. All makerspaces have their own cultures and amplify particular values over others, but the main components of a strong making culture are the opportunities to identify constraints, to play and experiment, to create a sense of community, and to have a sense of purpose, such as solving a problem and building entrepreneurial skills.

The Maker Mindset

When she was in school, Mary Beth Hertz, the director of education at Friends Select School in Philadelphia, was never introduced to the idea that girls could do tech, nor was she encouraged to pursue a career in STEM. But she grew up watching her dad work with technology, which both nurtured her natural curiosity and helped her not be scared of playing with tech, laying the foundation of her maker identity. "I wasn't scared of the black screen with a bunch of symbols on it," she said. "I always joke that I don't like to let technology win. Even if it's fixing a toilet, I like to figure out how things work and always have. And I'm not scared of fiddling with things."

Makers are not defined by their tools but by their mindset and process. Makers are often thought of as doers, but even within this focus on making and doing, there's a method to their madness. According to Dale Dougherty, founder of *Make* magazine, the maker mindset consists of the attitude of thinking about what can be done with what is already available, turning different ideas into various kinds of reality, undergoing an iterative process of improving a project, and participating in

MAKE
INSPIRATION

Foldit—How Gaming Culture Is Helping Scientists Understand Protein Folding

Scientists at the University of Washington have invited gamers with advanced spatial reasoning development to help them with protein biochemistry modeling. Made up of amino acids, proteins are the "workhorses" in every cell of every living thing. Although proteins are just a long chain of amino acids, they don't like to stay stretched out in a straight line. With Foldit, gamers can help scientists with protein structure prediction, as well as help design brand-new proteins that can prevent or treat serious disease. To learn more about Foldit, visit https://fold.it.

communities with like-minded people to share their work and expertise. Given Dougherty's perspective, makers don't need expensive things to be considered makers; they need to be resourceful and create out of their reality. Making is a form of self-expression that proves it's not the tools that define the maker, but the maker's ideas and their process of bringing their ideas to life.

The process of making something depends heavily on playing and experimenting with available materials while socializing with others who are embarking on the same shared mission. Unfortunately, though the capacity to make exists in all human beings, there are significant barriers that hinder a young person's ability to nurture this mindset. In education makerspaces such as those in schools, barriers can include grades, testing, insufficient time, classroom demands, and maker culture practices.[3] The true making mindset shifts the focus from obstacles to outcome, which requires the courage to take risks. However, classroom culture can play a detrimental a role in young people's ability to feel safe and supported enough to take creative risks. When society rewards and punishes based on test scores and earning grades, less emphasis is placed on making the time to experiment. Students from low-income households are disproportionately affected by losing access to quality education due to the punitive nature of the school system. Students from higher-income households are provided highly structured lives by their parents as well as by Advanced Placement courses, but as a result there is very little room to think on their own and to create. The luxury of authentic play to cultivate creativity and innovation is scarce in modern society. Everyone is just fighting for survival or chasing an image of success removed from their own humanity, instead of thriving in their genius.

Making enables students to free themselves from this paradigm. It enables kids to tinker, to fail, and to try again. There is no right or wrong way to make, and the spirit of making requires eliminating the confining idea of highbrow versus lowbrow. But the maker movement is not accomplishing anything new—making is inherently human. Supporting young people as makers is a way to help humans reconnect with their own humanity. Kids are naturally makers, but traditional schooling often drives it out of them. Our job as educators is to help students see themselves as makers, scientists, mathematicians, and artists so that they can claim these identities by speaking it to themselves. We can nurture this maker identity by providing students opportunities for agency and focusing on their strengths, by building a sense of community and purpose to solve a problem together, and by cultivating a culture that celebrates failures as opportunities to grow. We can give students the luxury of space and time to develop their naturally questioning minds. STEAM can feel off-limits to people who do not see themselves as good at math or who have never seen representation of their identities in STEAM fields, but the experimentation and openness of makerspaces, especially in the classroom, make STEAM accessible to everybody.

Making Matters

The maker mindset and identity are multidimensional. How makers demonstrate their skills amplifies some aspects of the maker mindset more than others, and the maker identity manifests in different ways depending on the culture of the environment in which the makers are cultivated. Maker cultures that emphasize competition reinforce a competitive mindset that focuses on winning, while cultures that focus on showcasing, such as at a Maker Faire, emphasize growth, learning, and sharing.

"Imagine that: a nation of innovation hobbyists working to make their lives more meaningful and the world a better place. Welcome to the maker revolution."

—Mark Hatch, CEO of Innovation Partners, author of *The Maker Movement Manifesto*

Great innovation occurs when people have the courage to take risks, and a large part of that courage comes from being comfortable with failing and making mistakes. Because the spirit of making focuses on play and experimentation, there is less emphasis on "doing it right" or "being perfect." There is no right way to be creative, and there is no failure in trying new things—other than not trying at all. When students learn how to fail forward—to learn from their mistakes rather than getting discouraged and giving up—they build resilience, which will help them bounce back from all of life's obstacles.

"Being encouraged from a young point to make mistakes and to experiment is fundamental," said Max Lawrence. "A lot of the best expressions of making stuff come from fantasy, meaning that you take the inputs of your experience in the world, and then those get processed, and then you can let go of judgment and produce something. And the reality is, a lot of times it turns out to be some sort of solution for something else. Being able to open up a channel into creating stuff, anything, be it music or art, really allowed me to become who I am now." Opening the channel of creativity that Max mentioned, letting go of self-judgment, and persevering when an idea doesn't work out—these are the keys to a lifetime of creativity and innovation.

There is an unfortunate and false notion of creativity in our culture that some people are just born more creative and brilliant than others. But creativity is not some special gift that's bestowed on a select few. It is not Newton getting hit on the head by an apple and then inventing calculus. Creativity springs from a breadth of exposure that often starts in one area, discipline, field, or context, and then a person makes the connection that, Hey, that could be useful in this other area that I'm working in or that a colleague or friend is working in. Having the space and culture that nurtures this kind of exploration and expansion is essential.

Creativity comes from practice and hands-on experience, and from allowing students to become explorers and to connect with other explorers. "The way you promote a creative society and culture is to expose more people to those explorers," says Youngmoo Kim. "More students expose more of the public to the breadth of these intersections and how they are meaningful and impactful." Making nurtures creativity through exposure, connection, and giving students the opportunity to create.

Making has built into it the multiple competencies required for entrepreneurship, which are often skills that aren't necessarily covered in schools—creating and finding value in something new, taking a risk on it, and creating change. It makes STEAM tangible in practical, useful ways as young people develop their own business ventures to sell their innovative products and ideas.

What's even more powerful occurs when projects like this are built through partnerships with the community. When projects find life outside the school setting, students can see themselves using their skills in the real world. A great example is a "hackathon" that Mary Beth Hertz organized, during which student teams competed to build a website for a local nonprofit business. The kids learned website design and coding, met with the nonprofit to learn about its needs, and were able to *see themselves* as professionals. The winners ended up getting hired to build and maintain the company's website.

This is a crucial part of maker culture: collaboration and community building, which happen within the makerspace, as well as with outside partnerships. Such collaborative cohorts can include institutions such as schools and local and global organizations, places where makers learn from each other and apply their skills to sustain different types of activities that go beyond the makerspace.

In educational makerspaces, there are three main aspects of culture that affect student learning, according to student interest, real-world relevance, and community collaboration.[4] If these conditions are successfully met, they can foster a culture that nurtures the maker identity and enables students to internalize that identity. In this way, making has the potential for meaningful social change in the form of social entrepreneurship. Mary Beth Hertz told me about a "Shark Tank: Social Entrepreneurship" activity that she runs. (See the activities at the end of the book.) While engaging in this activity, Mary Beth's students developed a business that provides clothing for people with housing insecurity. "We're going to provide awareness about the problem," Hertz said of the clothing line. "But we're also going to help solve the problem by providing interview clothes and things like that for people in need." Not only did they make a product and learn how to build a business around it, but they also saw a social need in their community and figured out how to fill it. As we will explore more in the next chapter, this kind of social entrepreneurship has the potential to empower students to catalyze change, both in themselves and in their communities.

MAKE
TAKEAWAYS

- The maker movement is a global phenomenon that includes independent inventors, designers, tinkerers, craftspersons, and artisans and that is essential for fostering innovation and helping people move from consumers to creators.

- The main components of a strong making culture are the opportunities to identify constraints, to play and experiment, to create a sense of community, and to have a sense of purpose.

- The maker mindset is not dependent on tools and materials, but it can be hindered in school-based makerspaces by barriers such as grades, testing, insufficient time, classroom demands, and a culture that plays a detrimental a role in young people's ability to feel safe and supported enough to take creative risks.

- Making is inherently human, and supporting young people as makers is a way to help humans connect with their own humanity.

- Making nurtures collaboration, resilience, creativity, twenty-first-century skills, entrepreneurship, and social change.

DRAFTING THE VERSE

MAKING IS NOT JUST FOLLOWING A RECIPE on Pinterest or some DIY website. It is the transformation of dreams into a product that solves problems and builds communities. Making has the potential to give young people the hope and agency they need to make the world a better place. But it is not a matter of empowering the youth—they already have the power. Rather, cultivating a culture of making in which young people see themselves as makers and think like makers enables them to nurture their own unique powers. Through making, they can dream and truly see how they can create change.

But the movement lacks diversity.

The maker movement was born from an exclusive industry. "Let's face it," said Youngmoo Kim, director of the Expressive and Creative Interaction Technologies (ExCITe) Center and professor of electrical and computer engineering at Drexel University. "The maker movement is a tech hacker movement at its core, and tech is born of the most exclusive enterprise and industry that we can imagine. It's not only exclusive in terms of race and gender. These are the super-rich people who come from privilege, who have access to tech and go into tech. It is kind of absurd for us to think that making in that formulation is going to be any more democratized, inclusive, or open. It's an industry built on exclusion, and exclusion breeds exclusion."

He shook his head and continued: "The assumptions that we place from day one on our students are wrong. There are cultural and gender biases, and we basically promote those who fit the culture as opposed to looking for ways to expand the culture." Very often, makers are stereotyped as males, and teachers can unconsciously place many responsibilities of leadership on male students, overlooking female students. Teachers and leaders in any community can unintentionally, or intentionally, make assumptions about people's abilities and value in the community.

Makerspaces are more common in more affluent schools and districts, often in suburban locations, and makerspaces located in urban regions tend to receive less educational support per student than suburban counterparts. Likewise, Maker Faires, hackathons, and other maker events lack diversity and often exclude women and people of color. "As I walked the floors of the Maker Faire," Tim Bajarin writes, "I did not see one African American family in the crowds, and I only saw two Hispanic families with kids checking things out. I would say the majority of the families there were white, although I also saw a lot of Asian and Indian families with their kids. The Maker Faire is a great show, but the lack of folks from these two communities tells me that we in the industry and those in the Maker Movement need to find ways to get these groups of folks interested in being makers, too. Without the participation of everyone, regardless of race, the Maker Movement may not reach its full potential, especially here in the United States."[1]

Kareem Eduoard speaks of a similar experience at a Maker Faire, where there seemed to be two separate fairs. "I went to this maker expo and all the people of color were on the outside near the parking lot. Inside, they had Google and everyone else. But it was people from the Philadelphia area that were using found resources, scrap metal, leftover wood furniture and turning them into wonderful works of art. I saw one where they built their own autonomous robot. But they were using found

"As humans, we are all born curious. We are built to explore, to hack the world around us, to understand it. It is in our very DNA to try to improve our lives, to help one another, to make each generation better than the one before it. From birth, a spark is born within us that calls us to be makers, doers, agents of change."

—Dorothy Jones-Davis, PhD, executive director, Nation of Makers and Neuroscientists material. That stuff was put outside in a tent so when you walked in, you didn't even see it; you had to catch it on the way back. Everybody in that tent was a person of color."

Kareem has talked to women who have described the dominant culture of maker spaces as being about "boys blowing up robots," where women and their interests are pushed to the side. He used the example of fabric and textiles—girls are dismissed for doing crafts, while boys are celebrated for using innovative "smart fabrics." He said, "Any time you throw in some type of tech word, then we're totally cool with it if it's a man that's engaging in it. That's where I also tend to see this idea of equity access and social justice become very problematic." This is just one small example of how, if the dominant race and class doesn't have a hand in the product that's being produced or the curriculum that's being designed, that product or curriculum is left on the periphery.

The language and culture of makerspaces can often be inaccessible, even hostile, to people of color and women. "Even though the facade of it talks about equity, access, and social justice," Kareem said, "the language within the makerspace itself sounds completely different. Young women who I have interviewed said that there are inappropriate jokes; there's language that sometimes is inaccessible. There's geek culture. Geek and making culture tend to be intertwined. There tends to be very heavy white male sexist language that's being used. And it makes folks feel uncomfortable that they are not able to have cultural references and access to some of the discussions that are taking place."

The solution will not come from putting a Band-Aid on these issues. We cannot just make things pink for girls or call a project "urban" to reach students of color.

The Maker Movement Needs Diversity

Monoculture leads to a loss of balance and the depletion of nutrients in any ecosystem. When communities lack diversity, they cannot sustain themselves and eventually fall apart. Likewise, diversity in ideas and how they are manifested is essential for helping makers and making thrive. The maker mindset does not just represent the dominant culture. In fact, making is birthed from some form of lack or constraint within a community. All human beings have a drive to resolve issues that matter to them. However, when those in positions of power impose that power in a way that gives some people more access and power than others, we perpetuate disparities.

The choices we make are a reflection of our deep-seated beliefs, and reflecting on why we make the choices we do can be uncomfortable. A maker team needs to hold one another and the organization accountable for becoming more socially just. To redesign the making community, those whose voices are amplified must learn to listen and validate the experiences of those who are not in their position. A team must work together to create structures where all feel supported, and the slight inconvenience one might feel from having to choose alternative ways of problem solving or to make alternative word choices is nothing close to the level of code-switching and accommodating experienced by those who have been dismissed. Becoming more socially just is an ongoing practice, not a state of being.

There must be a community-wide understanding of the need to address implicit biases and to be critically conscious of whether the choices we make perpetuate systems of oppression, however uncomfortable those conversations might be. The good news is that makers are the poster children of persevering through discomfort to resolve an issue. In the end, the maker community will thrive with more innovative ideas and will come together to address problems from multiple perspectives.

A Diverse Movement Builds Community

Making has the power to create meaningful and impactful change for the betterment of the community. Projects arising from the community allow people from the community to work toward a higher purpose. Very often in low-income and chronically stressed communities, families are just trying to survive. Involving community members in making, however, provides an opportunity for them to learn essential skills for making an income while also improving the conditions of their communities by doing something they are passionate about. The beauty of entrepreneurship is that it is grass roots: it starts from the local community and puts resources back into the community, as opposed to a giant outside company using the community for its resources.

Maker Culture Celebrates Collectivism

While makerspaces can provide participants the opportunity to design and create for themselves, maker culture also celebrates collectivism, where the sum of the parts benefits members of the community in terms of both skill and sharing of knowledge.

Making has the potential to build community by creating teams of people with diverse skills and backgrounds. Sajid Iqbal tells of a six-month-long training program he designed with the support of the US embassy in Bangladesh called the Renewable Energy Innovation Hub. "When I was working to solve different problems," he said, "I met a lot of students from reputed universities who were good at doing things practically, but I saw a gap between different professions like engineering students. They're not very curious. They are very good at math, they know how to calculate everything, but a lot of engineering students lack practical ideas on how to utilize these skills because they don't always get the opportunity to make impractical things and translate their skills into reality. So for the three months, I selected engineering students from different universities, I selected students from different polytechnical institutions, and I selected students from the community where we wanted to solve some problem. All these three groups came together to solve problems in the community, like lighting problems and water scarcity in rural areas, making a solar irrigation pump and streetlights out of simple things. I have seen when these engineering students and community people work together, they actually help each other with their different skills. They're sharing their skill set, and that actually helped us to make very simple, effective appliances within that period of time more efficiently and accurately. This kind of inter-exchange program helps gather interesting people to all work together, share ideas, and overcome their skill gaps and do something better."

The participants in this Renewable Energy Innovation Hub program were not only overcoming their skill gaps but also creating change within the community and solving real problems. The engineers Sajid worked with had been disconnected from the community and only had the experience of solving problems they found in textbooks. The project allowed them to develop agency and a new social competency, while the community members and other students acquired new technical competencies.

Sajid Iqbal—Bringing Light to the World

Sajid Iqbal is an environmentalist, innovator, and entrepreneur. Sajid founded Change, an organization that volunteered to install solar bottle lights throughout Dhaka, the capital of Bangladesh. Sajid aimed to first build a relationship with the community. The cultural approach he took included educating the families on the lower costs and greater efficiency of solar light sources. Sajid also focused on iterative design. When heavy rains caused leaks after the first bottle lights were installed, Sajid and team improved the design. The solar bottle project expanded rapidly across communities.

Maker Culture Gives Young People the Agency to Solve Real Issues

Many experiencing the empowering culture of making develop greater self-efficacy and a strong desire to apply their skills in the community. Young people really care about where the world is going and are more civic minded than ever. Supporting that natural passion is essential in nurturing the kind of citizens we need.

When young people are part of creating the solutions, they feel more engaged and connected to their communities. Two great examples are the Public Workshop and Tiny WPA (named for the New Deal Works Progress Administration) and their impact on cities' youth. The Public Workshop is an organization that helps youth and their communities across America address the very real issues they navigate daily. It partners with various institutions to grow and empower community-design leaders through projects that are youth initiated and community supported. The major curricular framework of the Tiny WPA program is that the participants of all ages identify constraints and then experiment with ways to solve the problems.

Flint, Michigan, is often portrayed in the media as a poor community with predominantly Black and Brown people struggling to get by, their suffering exacerbated by major environmental and public health crises.

Through opportunities provided by the Tiny WPA, Flint Public Art Project, Job Corps, and the Berston Bicycle Project, the young people of Flint are taking control of their city and sparking joy. Resources from these various institutions supported young people in building a playground on an abandoned property on Flint's north side. The playground is a place where kids and other community members can gather and enjoy themselves, and the project has been empowering for the young people who built the playground. In solving a real problem in the community, the youth are developing their maker mindset and their technical skills for building things as they make a positive impact. The youth of Flint are designing the community in which they live and spreading joy in a way that involves their community.

Making for Social Justice

Makers can lead the way to social justice. Innovative people have a tremendous amount of power that they can wield to create social change. In fact, the most impactful innovators are those who work toward social change and shape new cultural norms. Makers, entrepreneurs, and innovators are collectivists who are driven by the thirst to become better at what they do and work with their communities to find ever better solutions. Thus social justice is at the heart of making. Improving the systems in place to add value to one's community and be more inclusive of its people is essential for improving the maker culture.

Social justice embodies three core values: equal rights, equal opportunity, and equal treatment. Given this definition of social justice, the maker movement can continue to work toward becoming more socially just in how the culture operates, the ways of thinking it supports, and the products being made.

Makers play a pivotal role in designing systems for a more just society and inspiring the world to be better. For example, entrepreneurs aren't simply growing their businesses but are developing their ideas and adding value through the services they provide to their communities. Entrepreneurs are leaders who have the power to transform societal norms and can be role models for how companies can design systems to be more inclusive. Because entrepreneurs are self-directed, they are not confined to fit the mold of a higher authority. Entrepreneurs set their own standards of behavior and can take a stand and do what other

"Building isn't just about power tools, it's about power. We can change the authorship of the world."

—Emily Pilloton, founder, Girls Garage

businesses may deem controversial or are afraid to do. Their innovative mindset and culture enable them to revise and create new cultural norms, and their products and services can serve a greater social purpose that also has the potential to shift those norms.

Viewing a community with a deficit lens is detrimental to its well-being, as it disempowers the people of the community. Through making, the perception of the community is reframed to be more proactive so that communities that are often seen as impoverished and lacking can make innovative and useful things to support themselves and each other. We must challenge the assumption that those in power are the ones responsible for finding solutions. Members of the community, often led by its young people, are empowered by claiming responsibility for finding their own solutions.

Creative Solutions to Real Problems

Innovation is at the heart of human history, and often the most marginalized groups of people are the ones challenged to find creative solutions to their problems. Chaos can create space for people to gather and solve a collective issue. Many communities around the world are enduring challenging circumstances where groups of people are being marginalized, or lack access to resources that can enable them to meet their basic human needs. Yet, despite such challenges, there are makers and innovators who are able to look at what some may refer to as deficiencies in the community as opportunities to create change and move the community forward. Let's meet two of these makers.

William Kamkwamba

William is from Malawi and known as "the boy who harnessed the wind." He came of age during the famine of 2001, when he ate only one meal a day and had to drop out of high school at the age of fourteen. But hunger and lack of money did not stop him from going to the village library to continue studying. After exploring pictures of an electricity-producing windmill that was described as having the ability to generate electricity to pump water, he decided he would figure out how to make his own. Without any other instructions on what the windmill was made of or how it worked, William went to the junkyard and started experimenting with the scraps and spare parts. Finally, he made his own windmill, able to pump water to irrigate the dry fields of Malawi. Like many makers, William took what already existed to re-create it and revise it to meet the needs of his community.

Majd Mashharawi

Majd is a Palestinian civil engineer and entrepreneur who is applying her expertise to rebuild the Gaza strip while empowering her community through solar energy. In 2014, thousands of homes in Gaza were in ruins due to the war that has been raging for over a decade. After graduating college as a civil engineer, Majd focused on the need for building materials to rebuild her community. Women are gravely under-represented in the STEM fields globally, and although Majd was often discouraged from pursuing engineering, she took the discouragement as inspiration.

Majd did not have access to cement, aggregate, and sand, which are common materials used to make building blocks, and it was not feasible to try to import them into the war-stricken region. She started experimenting with various materials and discovered that she could mix the ashes produced from baking mud with the rubble of her broken city. After more than 150 failed experiments and over six months of research, her company, Green Cake, rose from the ashes and rubble of the demolished houses of the Gaza strip, using a building block that is cheaper and stronger than materials used before. Fresh college graduates from the area, especially female engineers, were hired to design and rebuild their community.

These innovators did not wait for someone outside their community to rescue them. These makers identified problems to solve in their community, figured out the constraints that would challenge them to think differently to solve the problem, found the courage to experiment and defy naysayers, collaborated with their community, gained access to other communities to gather resources, and created sustainable change. Instead of being discouraged by the lack within their community or aspiring to be like a different community, they reframed the lack of access as an opportunity to intervene and act. When they lacked the means or the tools, they reconceptualized the ways that readily available materials around them could be used.

Social Justice Is Maker Culture

The maker mindset is that of being resourceful, and even though inequities are very real, creating something for the community from materials found within the community, by people of the community, is empowering, and connects the learning space to the realities of the people who are to benefit from the products made.

To sustain a culture that is genuinely socially just, the makers of all walks of life need to prioritize critically analyzing power dynamics and acknowledging whose voices are heard and whose are dismissed or overlooked. If makers want to have real impact, they must reframe their relationship with the community from being a savior to being a comrade, working collectively with the community to improve the relationship. Therefore, representatives of the communities must be included in the process of making. People on the making team also need to be incentivized to undertake training on implicit bias so that they can better understand their own thought processes that affect how they interact with other people.

It is human nature to feel threatened when anyone suggests that what we are doing is wrong; however, it is also embedded in the maker identity to acknowledge one's own failings in order to become better. What distinguishes makers from others who are not risk-takers is that makers seek opportunities to fail and improve. Becoming a socially just human being is a making process. Instead of framing social justice as a separate trendy hashtag to increase a company's apparent palatability for current times, leaders in the making community must assess how the process of making and the products being made are equitable.

For making to increase social justice, educators must create opportunities for youth to take action and create change, intentionally dismantle power structures that exclude groups of people, reevaluate how to authentically include people (not just through lip service), address socioscientific issues, and engage citizens in resolving community issues. If we are able to do this, we can help empower young people to, as the famous saying goes, become the change they want to see in the world.

Making Your Classroom

Mary Beth Hertz and Max Lawrence are both experienced classroom teachers who are also makers, and they encourage educators to focus on developing young people's maker identity as opposed to fussing over the fancy laser cutter or 3-D printer. There is a common assumption that making needs to be expensive and use fancy tools, but tools cannot replace the creativity of human beings. Once young people have established what they want to create, then the tools can be an extension of their ideas. Hertz argues that as long as teachers are doing design thinking in their classrooms—where students are prototyping, solving problems, experimenting with materials to find solutions, communicating their ideas, and revising their process and products—then teachers are cultivating makers. Everyone, including teachers, needs to engage with the deep design thinking process; otherwise the classroom just becomes a "nice little factory that makes funny, cute stuff, and doesn't teach anything."

What You Need—and Don't

As I have mentioned throughout this section of the book, making is not new. Creating is the natural state of humanity. The tools, equipment, and materials are just extensions of what is innate in every student. In fact, focusing on the need for fancy equipment can sometimes detract from the authentic experience of making. Often high-need schools will get donations of old, broken equipment such as laser cutters, and they will be so focused on getting the thing to function that they lose focus on the actual work of creating. And, perhaps even worse, they fall into the mindset of believing they are dependent on outside sources. Students gain agency by finding—or making—accessible tools that can do the same thing as fancier gadgets.

Repurposing materials and navigating a lack of resources are inherent to the spirit of making, and we see it even in huge companies such as Nike, who is repurposing its sneakers to make new shoes. Kareem Edouard says that what needs to happen first, before any talk of being dependent on particular equipment, is that students should think about what they want to design and create, and then they figure out how to repurpose materials they can find within their communities to ultimately fulfill that design. He tells students about what Nike is doing as an example of even major corporations doing these same things. "And it is at that moment," he said, "that students start to think about themselves, not only as entrepreneurial individuals that have an opportunity to repurpose and redesign their communities, but they also start to realize something really simple. I don't need the fanciest pieces of equipment to execute something. What I need is a better understanding of the competencies that go along into designing and building, understanding how to manipulate the technical frameworks to make something happen."

Design Thinking

Rather than choosing equipment or specific projects, designers of new makerspaces should first consider the kind of learning culture they seek to create for their students. Don't just create a makerspace for the sake of having a makerspace; there must be a clear purpose and intentionality that is centered around the students. To engage students, makerspaces must gauge student interest, provide opportunities for collaboration, and adapt to the changing needs of the group.

Design thinking—an iterative process used to solve problems—can be employed to construct and cultivate those spaces. In this context, it's useful to think about design as a function of problem solving. What are the needs of the students, and how can design meet those needs? I spoke with Sam Seidel, the K12 Lab Director of Strategy + Research at the d.school at Stanford University, and he mentioned the concept of using space as another teacher, where we can use design as a pedagogical tool. His work with the d.school is a perfect example of how design thinking in a makerspace fosters creativity and innovation. You will not see the default sterile desks in rows at a d.school space. Its design is modular and movable, engages the senses, and offers entry for the multiple intelligences and diverse interests and abilities of the students. Every day, and for every project, teachers and students must be intentional about how they set up the space.

"A collection of tools does not define a makerspace. Rather, we define it by what it enables: making."

—MakerSpace community

Unstructured "Open Hours" and Open Curriculum

Students need the opportunity to explore and use the materials on their own time and on their own terms. Having unstructured time creates opportunities for students to become intrinsically motivated to do the work, without the pressure and stress of an assignment, grade, or ticking clock. Open hours benefit students who feel constrained by time, enabling more students to explore and use tools they do not have a chance to use during their structured class time.

Likewise, a more open curriculum enables students to engage with what matters to them, increases agency, and challenges them to innovate. It also supports inclusivity by allowing information to be presented in multiple domains. Formal learning spaces often use preconstructed lessons and kits, whereas informal learning spaces focus on self-directed projects. There is certainly value in predesigned curriculum, as students have "articulated that having detailed designs and creation processes reduced anxiety and provided a guided opportunity through new makerspace experiences."[2] Structured projects can be a great entry for many students and teachers who feel intimidated by making. However, students who participate in a more open curriculum model feel a sense of empowerment and agency due to the flexible nature of the curriculum. Both models serve a purpose, but the exploratory nature of the more open curriculum seems to embody the maker mindset, increase interest in doing the work, and cultivate creativity.

The Right to Make

Not all makerspaces are the same, and the design of the makerspace must adapt to the makers' needs and provide alternative pathways for learning. Makerspace participation can positively impact a broad range of students, but school leaders must be mindful to recruit inclusively, for both instructors and students. The most common framings encountered within internal school recruitment for makerspaces were "students who are a bit geeky and can innovate" and "smart kids who like to tinker." This declaration of a specific participant identity presents a potential barrier for broader inclusion in a makerspace. If kids do not already see themselves as "a bit geeky," as someone who "can innovate," or as a "smart kid," they will receive the message that this space is not for them. In an empowering and inclusive environment, the maker identity should be available and assigned to ALL students.

Teachers are in a position of power, and whatever power dynamic they create is often an extension of the power dynamic that has dictated society for generations. It is important that teachers reassess their relationship with power if they want to create a more inclusive and just world. Use your privileges as the teacher to give students access. Build a relationship with students in order to create a safe community where risk-taking and failing become norms, and where everyone works together to address a collective concern. Constraints are the seed of innovation, but it is a culture of accessibility and encouragement that can empower a student with the courage to imagine, believe, try, and persevere.

MAKE
TAKEAWAYS

- The maker movement was born from the exclusive tech industry and lacks diversity in terms of race, gender, culture, and class.

- Diversity is necessary for the maker movement to thrive, and each maker community needs to hold itself accountable for the ongoing work of becoming more inclusive and socially just.

- Makers are entrepreneurs who can work outside outdated and oppressive modes to transform social norms and be role models for other companies and organizations.

- Rather than operating from a deficit lens, makers can see potential for growth in a lack or need within their community and become empowered to make sustainable and meaningful change—for the community, from materials found within the community, by people within the community.

- Forget fancy gadgets like 3-D printers. Making is an inherently human endeavor. Focus on creating the time and space for students to experiment and innovate. Then be mindful of the fact that ALL students have the right to experience making and see themselves as makers.

VOLUME **4**

Dream

CHAPTER 8

Growing the Rhyme

THE GREATEST CHALLENGE to arriving at scientific and mathe-matical actualization (for ourselves and our students) is limitations on the imagination that are created by cultural norms that are more about an allegiance to the status quo than what is best for teachers and students. We do not grow or allow our students to grow when we cannot see beyond what we have been given and cannot act in ways that bring us the comfort to learn because they defy cultural norms. Culture can be loosely defined as the ways of knowing and being of a particular group of people. Cultural norms are the customs, rules, and traditions that guide a population.

In STEM, as described in volume 1, we have a distinct culture, and we enact particular cultural norms that reinforce the exclusivity of the subjects and the ostracization of those whom society sees as not belong-ing. More important, we have perceptions of what intelligence, academic success, and the path toward being a STEM professional look like that leave no space for a lot of children to imagine themselves as part of the STEM community. This culture of STEM teaching and learning leaves youth with no desire to join the community.

In communities across the country, the culture of STEM manifests itself in different ways, but with similar results. In urban and rural communities that predominantly assist underserved youth, STEM instruction is often more about complicity than anything else. Educators operate with an approach to teaching that couples the lack of access to resources with ensuring that young people are following strict rules, not questioning authority, and not playing too wildly. There is a perception that being STEM ready means being able to be controlled by teachers and do what you are told. STEM classes for these students involve cookbook labs where students are mostly given instructions to arrive at an expected outcome, rather than being allowed to manipulate resources and experiment to discover concepts and ideas. This is particularly the case for Black children in urban communities. Unsurprisingly, they're often the least likely to pursue careers in STEM. These students have had their learning so confined and scripted, they've been robbed of the opportunity to fully live, become, and dream.

In more affluent communities, where parents are preoccupied with making sure their children get into the best institutions of higher education and pursue careers in STEM, another type of dream robbery is taking place. These children's lives are so tightly packed with sports, music lessons, tutoring, and homework that there is barely time and space for them to play, discover, and dream.

If we're to increase equity, make the future better, and help kids live meaningful lives, we need to acknowledge how we are harming students with our present cultural norms and give them back the space to dream. Where can this happen on a regular basis? It can happen in any space where young people gather—especially in the classroom. With each opportunity to teach comes another opportunity to dream of new ways to connect and engage. In this process—where teachers are more innovative and creative about what they teach and how they teach it—teachers can model for students that creativity is privileged in the learning process. The right to dream is also returned at home when young people are allowed to play, invent, take apart, and build simply for the sake of doing so.

This is the work of creating a Dream Culture.

Dream Culture is about recommitting to the dream of thriving schools for the sake of our children's futures. It is dreaming of what is possible once students, faculty and staff, and community members all feel valued as vital stakeholders in the success of young people. Sometimes we get so caught up in linear thinking and just making it through all the stressful demands of our jobs as teachers that we lose sight of our values and why we entered the service as educators in the first place. This chapter invites us to construct a vision of a Dream Culture in our classrooms that benefits our students, as well as ourselves.

Encouraging Imagination

A Dream Culture is a lived reality that privileges a way of thinking and doing that pushes the boundaries of normality by encouraging the imagination and manifesting what it produces. To hold a Dream Culture is to sit with and channel our values in such a way that a symbiotic community is created where all are given what they need to become the best they can be. To hold such a culture in STEM is to pursue a world where all can engage with and have a command of these subjects as they fully understand who they are (inherently ingenious by virtue of existing) and want to be (realizing the full potential of this inherent genius).

A STEM Dream Culture pulses in transcendent rhythm, allowing members to freely explore their own dreams and how they can contribute to something greater than themselves. In the increasingly complex and global world we live in, comfort with and fluency in STEM are key to meeting the goal of contributing to something greater than ourselves. The core of Dream Culture is to activate our innate human instincts of ultrasociality—a unique and complex connection to one another enhanced in social spaces, such as classrooms, where we allow one another to fully be by welcoming expressions of culture in their varied forms. Ultrasociality thrives in classrooms where there is a beloved community. A beloved community, famously argued for by Martin Luther King Jr., is a space where justice, equal opportunity, and love of others, despite difference, are paramount. A STEM Dream Culture is the operationalizing of the concept of beloved community in pursuit of new languages that allow us all to comfortably enter new worlds.

A STEM Dream Culture is one in which the cultural norms are established by all those within the classroom and in which the rules of

"By nurturing the entrepreneurial spirit, students will see that they can create their own jobs and industries depending on their interests."

—Laura Fleming, library media specialist, author of *Worlds of Making* engagement are malleable. It is the recognition that for things to remain as they are is to subject someone to a reality they have had no part in creating and a world where they have been locked out. A Dream Culture is the exact opposite of the typical STEM culture we interrogated at the beginning of the book—a culture that tells someone that they are not a mathematician or scientist because who they are and how they engage in the world are not welcome in math or science.

The difference between a dream and a pipe dream in STEM is the work required to bring the vision to fruition. Dream Culture is the manifestation of dreams through the creation of norms that support more inclusive, engaging, and transformative STEM spaces, such as a makerspace, a collider classroom, or another space that values different cultural perspectives and provides the safety needed to experiment, make mistakes, and even fail. It is marked by classrooms with creative risk-taking, cooperative practice, collective citizenship, and cogenerative teaching experiences—a place where teachers and students coconstruct an environment in which all are comfortable as they become their best selves.

Purpose, Passion, Possibilities

We've all fielded this query in one form or another from an astute student: "What is the point of learning this? I mean, are we *ever* going use this in our real lives?" If you are a STEM educator, the question comes more often when the teaching is focused on a task that is not situated in real life or that is focused more on calculation than on conceptual understanding. When students question the instruction, it likely puts the teacher on the defensive. It may be interpreted as a shot at the teacher's pride and teaching ability. Many of us, in exasperation, have uttered the predictable answers that our students have come to expect: "This is something you need to know to pass the test." Or "Look, I didn't make the curriculum, but I have to teach it." Or even the most dreaded response: "Because that's just the way it is." This commonplace experience is a powerful moment for either fostering or killing Dream Culture. I reflect on the number of times I've heard this question from students and have given the responses here. What made me say these things? On some level, I probably agreed with my students' sentiments. I was defensive because I knew that I was protecting something I didn't believe in. The students were identifying a truth about the teaching that needed to be questioned.

When young people challenge what they are being taught, they are communicating a complex array of sentiments that can be hard to capture in the moment. First, they are telling you that they believe their time should be respected. They are also providing an opportunity for you to reimagine the instruction and start creating a Dream Culture. The reality is, young people hold a future-oriented and Dream Culture mindset that is not allowed to flourish in schools. The longer they endure classrooms where this approach is not allowed, the more they see the subject being taught as something separate from who they are and who they dream to be.

In addition, they're indicating that they want to learn but that this lesson isn't doing it for them. This is evidenced by the fact that many of us can think of days with those same classes where everyone is engaged, asking brilliant questions, and slow to leave when the bell rings. In asking this question, our students are saying, "I would absolutely give more effort to engaging with this if I saw how it could be useful to me."

Finally, they are communicating that a vast disconnect exists in the classroom—a rift that divides teacher from student. In this final point, the teacher represents a manifestation of everything students tend to find stifling about school: aloof paternalism, knowledge that isn't concretely applicable, and an unwavering demand for loyalty without granting it in return.

In essence, with this question, young folks are asking you, "Is this in tune with your values? Because it sure isn't aligned with mine." It shows that students care because they are attempting to interrupt a classroom environment that is benefiting no one.

Breaking Gravity

Many students from socioeconomically challenging backgrounds come to the classroom with broken dreams—a condition that emerges from having a home life that requires so much effort to get the bare essentials to survive that there is little space to activate the vision to dream and thrive. They do not get a choice in being able to dream because life automatically defaults to engaging in tasks for survival. This situation, coupled with a schooling experience that is driven by pursuing tasks (answering posed questions in a rigid cycle of consuming information and regurgitating it on structured assessments that do not measure

Dream INSIGNIFICANT

Dream INSPIRATION

Raven the Science Maven

Dr. Raven Baxter, also known as Raven the Science Maven, is an award-winning and internationally acclaimed science educator and molecular biologist creating science spaces that are inclusive, educational, and real. She is known for her unique musical teaching practices, combining hip-hop and science to engage the public. Baxter speaks about innovation in science education and social change in STEM. She is the creator and cohost of a STEM talk show, *STEMbassy*, and Black In Science Communication, a group that works to build relationships in the science community, equipping others with the knowledge and resources necessary to share science with the world in their own flavor. Baxter also owns Smarty Pants, a clothing company that sells fun and stylish STEM-themed apparel and accessories, and hosts an annual scholarship for STEM students. Check out her site to learn from and connect with her: www.scimaven.com.

anything but short-term memory and blind obedience), is a dream stealer that impacts the extent to which the brain trains itself to function optimally and engage in STEM.

The problem is that the view of STEM that is facilitated by Dream Culture rarely exists for kids. For many, they have other priorities in life or are experiencing some sort of trauma both within and outside school, spurred on by assaults on their sense of self and their beliefs about their abilities. For others, their lives have been overscheduled, taken up by tutoring, sports, lessons, or other supervised activities designed to make them more appealing as college candidates or to give some signal that they are smart or worthy of engaging in further study in the best institutions. In both cases, kids lack the space and time to dream, and the world suffers missing out on their genius.

The concept of time is essential. The truth is, we all make time for what we value. If we do not create space and time for youth to just be and make connections to content, we adults are telling them that we do not value their whole selves. Intentionally or not, we have then stolen their chance to dream.

The reason a lot of young folks do not get a chance to engage in STEM is that they are not provided with what I call the necessary luxury of the time to dream. When young people are essentially raising themselves, or raising other kids in their families, or working, or dealing with real-life issues, their bandwidth to dream becomes grievously limited. At the same time, there are thousands of young people who are the so-called winners of the game of school; they enter college, but they are brittle. Yes, they have worked hard. They received perfect grades and tested well. For them, it is very difficult to understand failure. This means that they rarely try to tackle ideas or tasks outside the box; they are afraid to think big.

Whether we are talking about the colonization of dreams by the structure of schools that limit what young people can dream about, or the robbery of dreams by socioeconomic realities that make it impossible to dream, the phenomena remain the same and their implications for who gets to engage in STEM are real. We have different isotopes of the same phenomenon in a system that has robbed young people of their dreams, of their opportunity to discover their purpose and grow into their potential. It is a rare phenomenon that is not a question of wealth or affluence or socioeconomic class or even, in this instance, race. Although it takes different forms with different people, it is the same process.

The question we must all ask ourselves is this: What sacrifices must we make to provide all young people with that necessary luxury to dream?

How do we understand that what we may have historically perceived of as a luxury—time to play, time to think, time to make connections, time to dream—is actually a need? If we want to protect the potential of our children, our work moving forward must be to sacrifice for the necessary luxury of dreaming. To do this, we must ask ourselves, How do we ensure that classrooms not look or feel like places that imprison the body? How do we make the science lab feel like a place of comfort—one that sets the mind and heart free in the pursuit of knowledge and the leveraging of this knowledge for doing good work for others? How do we break the gravity of students' current environment, whether that environment is uncertain and insecure or rigidly ambitious?

We all have been conditioned to believe that being busy and having an insurmountable set of tasks to complete equate to worth, to value, or to smartness. But should students wonder whether they are smart

"Once students are able to incorporate the arts and their culture into the science content, they take it and they run with it."

—Chris Emdin

enough to take a STEM course because their score on that last standardized test was disappointing? Should we let them doubt their abilities because they didn't "finish their work" in class today? There's a certain unkindness toward the self being expressed and maintained by a culture of immediacy that reflects our task completion–driven culture. The work of educators who truly want young people to connect to STEM is to offer them the space to dream in school. This includes being explicit about the ways that the concept of dreaming is not just part of the classroom but also part of academic discipline.

Dreaming is what great scientists have done for a very long time. Dreams and imagination are what spur on the scientific enterprise. Every one of my favorite stories about scientific inventions begins with dreams. August Kekulé, who has been described as one of the most important scientists of all time because of his contribution to the theory of chemical structure, once mentioned that he discovered the ring shape of benzene in a daydream he had of a snake biting its own tail. Einstein's scientific contributions were all rooted in his "thought experiments" and vivid imagination. We come to understand relativity because he imagined running beside a light beam. In addition, although this is not discussed often, he began engaging in thought experiments after attending a Swiss village school based on the educational philosophy of Johann Heinrich Pestalozzi, who believed in encouraging students to visualize concepts. Einstein attended this school after he left his more traditional school, where he was stifled by rote learning and the rigid structure.

There is a brilliant song titled "Dreams" by the rap group Little Brother. It has a mesmerizing chorus: "Mama I have dreams, but dreams don't keep the lights on." The refrain, powerful in its simplicity, describes the experiences of a child telling his mother that he has dreams that are bigger than what she wants for him. But he also realizes that dreams will not pay his light bill. The message is that without the dream, his light— his artistry, his passion, his purpose—couldn't stay on. Dream Culture in STEM and STEAM is about the space to explore one's thoughts and STEM ideas in a way that keeps our inner light for learning turned on.

I understand that some may question how we achieve these STEM dream goals in a world so rife with discord and a school culture so committed to maintaining the status quo. I argue that while a beloved community and a Dream Culture may be hard to attain in the world, they are absolutely possible in the classroom. Every classroom can be a microcosm of the world we want to live in, instead of a replication of the world we have. Whatever it is you seek in education or beyond, it can be realized when a Dream Culture, and its concomitant collective state of uplift, exists.

It is also important to understand and share with students what happens when we deny ourselves the right to engage in Dream Culture—when we deny them and ourselves a deep connection with our instinctual yearning to be ultrasocial. In denying Dream Culture, we deny purpose. In denying Dream Culture, we deny transcendence. We enter a state of perpetual "dream deferral" and never emerge from it.

Dream Culture in the STEM classroom cannot be operationalized without the acceptance that the perfect classroom is "always becoming." We never arrive at the ideal classroom. It is a perpetual work in progress embarked on only when all students are fully visible and fully authentic. Students participating in a Dream Culture must be reminded daily of their value to the community and of the power of exploring their dreams. It is only when they dream individually and collectively that we can create a beloved community. In many ways, students reflect the purest sense of becoming, in that their scholastic experience exists in theory to nourish their inquisitiveness and hunger for exploration. Perhaps that is why many of us entered this field, as we felt the call to concretely contribute to the edification of our youngest generation.

Dream
TAKEAWAYS

- Dream Culture is about recommitting to the dream of thriving schools for the sake of our children's futures. It is dreaming of what is possible once students, faculty and staff, and community members all feel valued as vital stakeholders in the success of young people.

- To hold a Dream Culture is to sit with and channel our values so that all students are given what they need to become the best they can be. This is a space where justice, equal opportunity, and love of others, despite difference, are paramount.

- Young people naturally hold a future-oriented, Dream Culture mindset that is not allowed to flourish in schools. The longer they endure classrooms where this approach is not allowed, the more they will see the subjects being taught as something separate from who they are and who they dream to be.

- The view of STEM that is facilitated by Dream Culture rarely exists for kids. For many, they have other priorities in life, or they're experiencing some sort of trauma. For others, their lives have been overscheduled, taken up by tutoring, sports, lessons, or other supervised activities. In both cases, kids lack the space and time to dream, and the world suffers missing out on their genius.

- Although a Dream Culture may be hard to attain in the world, it is absolutely possible in the classroom. Every classroom can be a microcosm of the world we want to live in, instead of a replication of the world we have. Whatever it is you seek in education or beyond, it can be realized when a Dream Culture, and its concomitant collective state of uplift, exists.

CHAPTER 9

Laying the Track

LELAND MELVIN IS A BRILLIANT ENGINEER and former astronaut who served on board the space shuttle *Atlantis*. When I interviewed Leland for this book, he shared one of his most life-changing experiences with me. When he was young, Leland's father came home one day in an old, beat-up bread truck. Once his dad had limped the wheezing truck into a parking spot, he told Leland that it would be the family's new recreational vehicle. Leland couldn't believe it. The truck looked useless. "He said, 'This is our camper," Leland told me. "But I said, 'No. It says Merida Bread and Rolls right on the side.'" Nevertheless, his father convinced him that there was something beyond what Leland could see. Under the wear and tear, his father told him, there was potential in the truck; under the faded paint and grease, there was a kind of magic. As Leland explained, "He had a vision for the truck—and for his family."

Slowly, over time, his dad built up the truck. He fabricated a bed and drawers. He painted it bright red, adding a new glimmer of life to the rusting hulk. He added small gadgets: a lamp, a two-burner stove, a compass, and a radio. Leland helped him with the process. As they worked, they sometimes talked about the truck, but they often talked about the importance of family, friends, and purpose in life. Before long, they had an amazing vehicle that the family used to travel across the country on vacation. To this day, Leland still vividly remembers this experience—the hard work, the conversations, and the lessons learned.

This story, in its elegant simplicity, is the essence of good teaching. It presents something (a concept, an idea, a problem) to students even if they feel no connection to it (or see it as ugly or too hard) and then invites them to see possibilities that they can enjoy or be part of. What inevitably happens during this experience is that young people will have some apprehension. The role of the STEM or STEAM educator here is to find out what the emotion is that inhibits the student from working on the truck. In other words, what is blocking them from seeing the potential or magic in a concept or project? What is preventing them from seeing the dream? This process, like Leland's experience, creates indelible experiences and enduring moments.

Researchers in different fields refer to these types of moments or experiences in different ways. Some call them peak moments or peak experiences. Others refer to them as moments of flow. Sociologist Emile Durkheim called the concept *collective effervescence*—a situation in which a community or society comes together with like mind and focuses on pursuit of a shared vision. I suggest that teaching within a Dream Culture is about the pursuit of this collective effervescence that the teacher and the learner share—one that transcends the moment and connects the teacher, the learner, and the content in ways that shape their identity or their perception of self.

From Worship to Belief

Collective effervescence is reached when all human beings in a particular place are operating with shared goals and ideals in ways that do not occur in everyday life outside that place. Emile Durkheim referred to religious gathering spaces where people congregate and express shared emotions, and "an electricity is generated from their closeness and quickly launches

"Kids are born scientists."

—Neil deGrasse Tyson, astrophysicist, cosmologist, planetary scientist, author, and science communicator them to an extraordinary height of exaltation."[1] Whether in the home or the classroom, you develop scientific or mathematical identity by attaching the engagement with these subjects to this innate, collective sense of joy—to a shared experience that invokes an unparalleled euphoria and a desire to learn and do more.

Most people rarely experience moments or times of collective effervescence and only get to witness them in glimpses as individuals reach peak performance. A basketball player who hits shot after shot is described as being in the zone. A boxer who dodges a number of punches in a row or an actor who slips so deeply into a character that she becomes the role has reached a level of peak performance that we all get to witness. These are times when an individual is operating at their full potential in the pursuit of a task or goal, and it's magical to witness.

When Michael Jordan hit six three-pointers in a row in the 1992 NBA finals or when Muhammad Ali dodged twenty-one punches in ten seconds against Michael Dokes in 1977, the world stopped to bear witness to a human being achieving individual greatness. Their performance is so seamless—both extraordinary and effortless—that they almost seem to be in another reality. And they are: they're in a dream state.

The truly fascinating thing about these moments, however, is the emotion that is generated from the thousands of people who are witnessing it. These people, who feel the chills from the moment, are all collectively experiencing something special. Oftentimes that feeling is allowed to slowly dissipate and then translate into some type of hero worship.

I argue that it doesn't have to be this way.

Good teaching brings together those who have experienced something powerful. It connects all those who witness a certain magic in an appreciation for what they have witnessed. Then it pulls them into seeing themselves not as observers of the magic but as participants in it. This is what the creation of a Dream Culture does—it pulls all students into this experience of joy.

The interesting thing about collective effervescence is that one individual operating at peak performance can invoke it; so can the pursuance of peak performance by the person who was previously only peripherally engaged. This is what teaching science, math, or any other "technical" subject requires: educators who are deeply in tune with their full emotional and physical selves operating in their own dream state, introducing young people to such an experience and then generating the collective effervescence in the young people that invokes their own pursuit of seeing, dreaming, and being.

This type of collective effervescence offers young people the chance to push themselves, discover an identity, collaborate, communicate, and take on leadership roles—all in a safe space and with relevant outcomes. The entire enterprise of moving toward this collective effervescence requires a Dream Culture. Dream Culture creates the environment for joy, for these moments and experiences to happen.

Not just for some students but for *all students*.

Even KE = $\frac{1}{2}$ mV^2 Can Seed a Dream

I walked into the classroom, gave the students a warm-up question, and then scribbled two formulas on the board: PE = mgh and KE= $\frac{1}{2}$ mV^2. These formulas were as ugly to ninth graders who had never taken algebra as that old bread truck was to young Leland Melvin. I saw lines in brows almost immediately. Looks of confusion spread across the room. From somewhere in the room I heard, "What in the world does that mean?" This simple question seemed to capture the essence of what almost all the students felt. I was Leland's dad pulling into the driveway with the old truck that meant nothing.

I knew that these formulas—for potential and kinetic energy—apply to many powerful concepts in science. My job, therefore, was to show these students the shiny, fun-filled RV within the wheezing bread truck. I immediately told them that these formulas could be used to design playgrounds with basketball courts, and balloon-powered cars that could be templates for high-speed trains. Once I was able to have them see what I saw and show them what these formulas help us to understand, I was able to introduce my students to a design and creation activity that included designing a racetrack and ended with a balloon-powered car race that brought the concepts of potential and kinetic energy to life.

Now, they didn't just *need* to understand the ugly formulas; they *wanted* to understand them to improve their track designs and their balloon cars. True learning happens in moments like these, when the imagination is activated and the students forge powerful relationships with content. Most important, it is in these moments that students'

Dream INSPIRATION

LEGO®—The Building Blocks of Imagination

LEGO is a Danish toy production company best known for its sets of interlocking plastic bricks. The company was founded in 1932 by Ole Kirk Christiansen. The name *LEGO* is derived from the Danish words *leg godt*, meaning "play well."

For a classroom activity that uses toy building bricks, see the activities section at the end of the book.

perceptions of STEM disciplines shift, and they start seeing themselves as scientists and mathematicians, as designers and engineers. This is the case both for those engaging in the activity and those who are observing it.

As a former physics teacher, I have witnessed the fear that students bring to the classroom. After battling this absence of self-confidence and noticing the ways it stopped students from learning, I decided a few years ago to always suspend teaching content in favor of uncovering the beauty and magic of the subject and revealing the genius the students hold within.

Often, I began with introducing the content as it was—concepts that often seem as ugly as an old bread truck. I then introduced what it could be, the magical result or outcome it could be used to create. This is like Leland's dad introducing the recreational vehicle. I tell the story of what the subject could be and how beautiful it actually is despite what I drove up (walked into) the driveway (the classroom) with.

The next process is finding out whether students think the dream is worthwhile. Can they see it? Can they imagine what it could be even if it is not in front of them? If the students cannot see the dream, our job as teachers is about bringing it to them—creating a model of it and describing it in detail. If the dream still seems obscure, the work is to unearth their own dreams. Find their "ugly truck" and help them understand how it can drive them to their dream. It is through this process of pursuing the dream—when the student is conceptualizing, creating, doing, and making—that they achieve a state of joy, and true learning happens.

"Education is not memorization. It is the activation of the imagination and a path towards liberation."

—Chris Emdin

Space to Think and Dream

Every powerful teaching moment I have had—the ones when the entire class transitioned from being introduced to a new, complex concept to witnessing peak performance, and then to engaging in the formula for joyful learning, we were all so in touch with what we were learning that it created a type of nimbleness. To be nimble is to be quick, light, agile, and joyous. These are moments where the rules or conventions in place are there only to be pushed back against because the moment that is being created cannot be confined to the norms. For the basketball player, the rule that dictates not taking too many shots gets thrown out of the window in favor of doing what feels right.

When I taught physics, the most magical teaching moments were born out of statements such as, "Let's go play in the park today" or "Let's make a model of that and play in the hallway." These invitations to create, experiment, and make ended up as deep interrogations of the relationships among science and design, art, architecture—and life. There is a direct relationship between the extent to which students are given the space to play and the depth or rigor of the academic conversations they engage in.

The point here is this: children must be given the space to think, dream, and work in order for them to learn.

The work of our students is to question, to discover, and to dream. And our job as educators is to provide them with the contexts to make their experience productive. The full understanding of any scientific or mathematical concept requires the context that facilitates a dream. Once this dream becomes tangible, it can merge effortlessly with academic content. For example, a lesson around forces acting on an object only gets fully experienced and understood while students are on a tire swing and trying to get it to stop, as friends stand around on either side pushing at different times with different amounts of force. Students photograph themselves on the swing. They record video of the game. They pose questions to each other about how they got the tire swing to stop. Then all the information they gather—the experience, the recording, the questions, the laughter, and the joy—gets brought back into the classroom and activates a connection to the subject that cannot be made in the hyper-traditional classrooms.

This is the collective effervescence created through a Dream Culture.

Dreams Deferred, Dreams Unrealized

Considering the concept of collective effervescence, it is essential that we understand that the low numbers of students graduating with STEM degrees and the high numbers expressing disinterest in these subjects are directly related to the absence of a Dream Culture in our classrooms and the implementation of a dream-deferred approach to STEM instruction. The dream-deferred approach is one that convinces young people that not enjoying science or math or struggling through it is a requirement for working in science, mathematics, or related fields.

The concept of a dream-deferred culture is powerfully captured in a poem by Langston Hughes. In "Harlem (A Dream Deferred)," Hughes laments that unfulfilled dreams will dry up, fester, or crust over. He grieves for dreams that are perpetually delayed until they die. This raises a critical question for all of us: Are dreams really dreams if they are never pursued?

This is what happens when young people, with immense potential to change the world, are derailed from seeing possibilities for themselves because they either are not introduced to the skills they need to find their path or have a subject presented in such a way that it pushes them away from even wanting to dream. In too many classrooms, this looks like an environment that prematurely stops the joy that creates dreams. Schools that consistently present STEM subjects as a torturous path toward a joy that can only be attained *after* students have left school are also creating a school where students learn to not like these subjects. The narrative is that students should suffer in science and math classes until they get a job that pays well and that this job and the money it provides will make them happy.

There are a couple of problematic assumptions about this very popular belief. The first is that making money or getting paid well equates to joy. We all know that this is not always the case. There are many people who are in professions that pay well, but who are miserable due to a lack of purpose or passion. The other problematic assumption is that learning STEM subjects should feel like punishment or should be painful. This delaying of the dream in order to see who can withstand rigidity and the absence of joy in STEM classes is not just disheartening—it's devastating both to individuals and to broader society. Just think of how much potential has been lost at the gratuitous altar of stoicism. Finally, our culture of "winnowing" students—rooted in pushing out a large number of those who are pursuing STEM for the sake of retaining just a few who think only a certain way—is equally destructive to our individual dreams and our collective potential. Learning—and dreaming—in all forms should be encouraged, cultivated, and rewarded.

For far too many young people, the conditions of their classrooms rob them of an opportunity to live STEM dreams. A culture that demands struggle for survival gives little space for the affirmation and experience—the play—they need to activate the genius that lies in wait within them. Yes, a lot of our students hit our doors with deferred dreams. But our overwhelming infatuation with outputs without a consideration for fostering the creative space for the inputs leads to a stifling of discovery, joy, and imagination. We have lost imagination because we no longer dream. And when we don't dream, we don't grow.

Dream Culture and collective effervescence offer a new approach to STEM that looks at education in these disciplines not as a subject to pass or fail or as a means to an end, but as a lifelong process. Dream Culture in STEM requires a recognition that we are all learning, dreaming, and becoming—and, yes, this includes the adults in the room. The next step for many of us is to understand that we can create this type of culture through self-excavation and the power of play. These are the tools we can use to bring a Dream Culture back into our schools and back into ALL students' lives.

Dream
TAKEAWAYS

- Teaching within a Dream Culture is about the pursuit of a "collective effervescence." Collective effervescence is reached when all human beings in a particular place are operating with shared goals and ideals in ways that do not happen in everyday life outside that place.

- When collective effervescence is achieved, the imagination is activated, and students forge powerful relationships to content. In these moments, students' perceptions of STEM disciplines shift, and they start seeing themselves as scientists and mathematicians, as designers and engineers.

- Children must be given the space to think, dream, and work in order for them to learn. Their work is to question, discover, and dream. Our job as educators is to provide them with the contexts that make their experience productive.

- The "dream-deferred" approach, all too common in schools, convinces young people that struggling through STEM subjects is a requirement for working in science, mathematics, or related fields.

- Dream Culture and collective effervescence offer a new approach to STEM that looks at education in these disciplines not as a course to pass or fail, or a means to an end, but as a lifelong process that brings joy.

CHAPTER 10

Mixing and Mastering

ABOUT TWENTY TEENAGERS STOOD BACKSTAGE in groups of two to four holding hands, pacing back and forth, and reciting lines to themselves. One of them stood on his own in a corner holding an invisible microphone in his hand, performing to an empty wall. There was an electric energy in the dimly lit and narrow hallway where they stood shielded from the crowd on one side of a thick black curtain. On the other side, a two-thousand-person auditorium was filled to capacity. A DJ stood as the lone figure on a dimly lit stage. He ran his hand across one of the two turntables in front of him shouting phrases that only seemed to build the excitement in the room with each utterance. Suddenly, he lowered the volume on the thick bassline of the rap song that had just been bouncing off every wall in the room. There was complete silence until he yelled, "Are you readyyyyyy?" in a deep and commanding voice that floated across the room just as the stage lit up. "Are you ready for . . . science!!!!!!"

This was the opening to the Science Genius BATTLES (Bring Attention to Transforming Teaching, Learning and Engagement in Science) initiative I started close to a decade ago. The initiative is focused on the intersections of science and hip-hop. Its chief goal is to create spaces for young people to bring into science the same passion and fervor they have for hip-hop. The entire initiative, which has been adopted in cities across the country, was birthed from my work coaching science and math teachers across the country and the powerful insight that work gave me into the conditions of STEM classrooms. One afternoon, after watching a class of high school students bored in their science classroom, and then seeing those same students express excitement and joy when performing raps for each other after school, I began to imagine what a different type of science experience could be for young people. That vision transformed into a science competition that charged young people with creating raps or poetry based on what they are learning in science class. I then created competitions in classrooms, schools, and eventually across cities rooted in the hip-hop ethos of love, unity, and having fun. Check out the event and the movement: hiphoped.com/science-genius.

A STEM Disaster

The creation of Science Genius came from seeing the ineffectiveness of the environments where young people were forced to learn. Students were disengaged, disinterested, and responding to STEM lessons with emotions that ranged from anger to frustration. These classes ended up with students not liking science or math or declaring that they were not good at these subjects. It was clear to me that STEM instruction for most young people was a disaster. The sending of resources to schools that purchased technology and built laboratories but didn't create STEM-minded young people appeared to be an utter failure.

The disengagement of our children from those who teach STEM must be corrected. It is not enough to mention that no one group operated with malicious intent to get us here—we must all recognize that our young people are not disposable. History has taught us that when we ignore and abuse our best resources, and do not invest in sustaining

Dream
INSPIRATION

Victoria Richardson—Science Genius Rapper and Columbia University Student

Victoria Richardson and her teammates were finalists at the Science Genius BATTLES (Bring Attention to Transforming Teaching, Learning and Engagement in Science). In the competition, Victoria and her team faced off against other science student-rappers from nine different New York public schools. The competitors wrote and performed rhymes about everything from gravity to energy to DNA to evolution. At the citywide finals, teams were judged by a panel that included GZA, a founding member of the Wu-Tang Clan.

"Science is something I always failed, which prevented me from getting into the specialized high school I wanted to go to," Richardson said. This changed for her through Science Genius. She has recently finished her student teaching work and in is now enrolled at Teacher's College, Columbia University.

and growing them, we run the risk of not only losing them but losing the best of ourselves.

To improve the conditions of STEM and learning in the US, we must first acknowledge and sit in the disaster we have created. Without reckoning with our mismanagement of students' dreams and potential, we cannot improve STEM. Reckoning is then followed by recommitment to our core values. After recommitting, we must reimagine—dream wildly and boldly, and not rest on the laurels of our past accomplishments but move diligently toward creating a better world. Science Genius was but one exemplar of the reckoning, recommitment, and reimagining model. I am not arguing for everyone to create science raps with students (though that wouldn't be a bad idea). I'm merely suggesting that it can serve as a model for how schools and teachers can look beyond the classroom to find new models for engaging students. The process is straightforward: identify a challenge to students' learning, look for solutions outside the place that created the problem, and then offer new solutions that magnify the gifts of young people.

I argue that reckoning, recommitting, and reimagining is impossible to accomplish when we are preoccupied with blaming parents, schools, administrators, and young people for current conditions. We all must start taking responsibility for changing the conditions of STEM teaching and learning. We must accept that we all have experienced too many situations where we have been complicit with norms that cause young people to be robbed of opportunities to uncover their mathematical and scientific genius. We must also accept that we will not address this reality without the proper societal will and recommitment to core values around having all young people reach their full potential and be scientifically and mathematically actualized—operating from and living at their fullest potential and utilizing STEM as a significant piece of their self-discovery. We must also recognize that an educator who is not working actively toward self-discovery cannot teach young people to do the same. This means that the first step toward creating a Dream Culture is to reflect on your own values and dreams.

Self-Excavation and Reflection

How often do we dig deep into the rich soil of self-introspection and reflect on the values and convictions that brought us to serve as educators? Do we ever sit with the ways that we are viewed in society and by scientists and engineers because we choose to teach? Do we really understand the call to teach and why it is important? Do we understand the significance of teaching science in a world where science holds so much status? Without our considering these questions, our actions are guided by other people's perceptions of the role of a teacher, and we are unable to achieve peak teaching moments.

As a person who spent most of his postsecondary training in the sciences, I have met a number of people who work in STEM. Over the years, many of them have become my friends. This group of friends includes a neuroscientist, a few engineers, a statistician, and a few others who are researchers. For years, each time that we would get together, we would all give updates on how we were doing professionally and reflect on our work. For years, whenever we would meet and I would describe what I was doing in the classroom, the tenor in the room would change.

"We would teach math so differently if we thought of math as play not as performance."

—Francis Su, mathematician, Benediktsson-Karwa Professor of Mathematics, Harvey Mudd College

The general sentiment was that what I was doing was not as significant as what my friends did. Questions like "Are you still doing the teaching thing?" would always come up. As soon as I said, "Yes," I would get a response that was somewhere between sympathy and "Good for you for being of service."

For years, I never knew what that feeling—the collective sympathy—meant. The "How nice of you to do that" statements and the condescension wrapped in kindness that was hurled at me for helping kids love science didn't sit well with me. I couldn't name the emotion until I did the work to think back about my initial connection to teaching science.

When was the moment I knew that this was what I wanted to do?

How did this become my dream?

The process of asking these questions of ourselves is one that requires a reflection and introspection that are the seedbed for the emotional release. It is the inner reflection that I call "innervisions." When activated, these innervisions allow us to live out Dream Culture in the key of life.

Whatever our innate values may be, it is fair to say that we educators are not often granted much time to step back and reflect on them. How does our pedagogy uphold or fall short of our deeply held values? What about the flow and layout of our classroom? The way we perceive our relationships with our students? The reason why we get up and go to work every day?

As you allow yourself the space to remember your teaching dreams and values, model that introspection with students and then ensure there is space for them to go through the same process. Values—and the dreams they shape—are the central forces that drive us. A connection to them is vital in maintaining our self-efficacy and spirit of becoming. In fact, conscious connection and alignment to values is an influential factor in allowing our students to mentally disarm the negative mindsets and stereotypes they face in STEM, STEAM, and school as a whole.

When teachers and students are unified in a connection to their individual and shared values, they embody Dream Culture. The culture catalyzes the actions and phenomena we hold to be the gold standards of classroom excellence: creative risk-taking, cooperative practice, collective citizenship, and cogenerative teaching experiences.

Even though there are many factors that can lead to a sense of overwhelm in our field, allowing ourselves and our students the space to reconnect with core values sets the foundation for the creation of a Dream Culture—one that engages the full spectrum of learning strength that exists within our young people and ourselves. In addition, sitting in critical reflection is often uncomfortable because it forces us to confront our imperfection, something typically discouraged or considered taboo in the "no negative vibes here" perfectionism culture that permeates many spaces. I argue that self-compassion is essential here. We all have days and moments of which we are not proud—times when, in retrospect, we plainly see that we were out of alignment with our values.

My encouragement to you is that the very act of recognizing these moments is one of immense empowerment because you can now learn from them. The ability to consciously reflect on an interaction or to realize that something about your classroom culture feels out of step is the key essence of a great educator. Furthermore, self-reflection doesn't need to be limited just to you. Once you model and demonstrate the importance of self-reflection to your students, they are often motivated to take the risk to do the same. This is a key step toward creating a true Dream Culture in your classroom.

Play More

STEM is play. STEAM and making are play.

Dreaming is play.

Play is the activation of parts of the mind that have often lain dormant for far too long. It is the driver of exploring, questioning, feeling, and making meaning as one operates in the key of life. For our students, it is essential that we protect play, especially free play. In contrast to organized play—such as games or activities directed by adults—free play is an opportunity for children to make the rules and leverage their imaginations without interference. It allows them to try out adult roles that they have observed or to practice skills that they want to work on, such as safely navigating obstacles or climbing, or skills they have been learning in more structured environments, such as sports. Children have full freedom to consider limitless possibilities in this mode.

Simply put, free play is the embodiment of dreaming in action.

Dream
INSPIRATION

DownCity Design—Building Play Structures and Learning Spaces

DownCity Design is a community organization working to develop local problem solvers. They empower students, educators, and community members to use design skills to improve the places where they play, learn, and DREAM. DownCity Design was founded by Adrienne Gagnon and Manuel Cordero, with the mission of improving the state of Rhode Island by getting young people involved in designing and building solutions for their communities. Since its founding, DownCity Design has grown rapidly, transforming the lives of young people across the state. This outdoor classroom is a great example of a Dream Culture space that they have created.

Nobel Prize–winning chemist Joachim Frank vividly remembers that playing in the rubble of his war-torn hometown after World War II was the trigger for his imagination and his appreciation for making meaning. His resulting ability to create order out of seeming chaos has made him the scientist he is today.

Free play gives children a safe space to learn some of the most critical and often most difficult social skills, such as leadership, sharing, equity, emotional regulation, executive functioning, negotiating, problem solving, critical thinking, and forming connections in creative ways. It makes them scientists and mathematicians, without naming them as such. Ironically enough, free play helps our young people build the very skills that educators point out are so often missing in the higher grades.

Play also gives adults a window into the mind of a child, especially those who may struggle to verbalize their thoughts and feelings because of anxiety or other barriers. It allows a young person to act out, in a safe environment, something that has been on their mind. Adults can leverage this understanding to enter conversations with the child in a more informed manner—it is one of the best forms of social and emotional learning!

The benefits of play extend to all age groups. It is one of our oldest and most intuitive forms of learning. During play, the imagination that has been colonized by school and its rules is now opened to free thought and expression. Appropriateness and its subtle way of holding us back are erased. There are no boundaries in place to confine the imagination. It is finally set free.

Altogether, this makes a compelling case for how schools and society should revisit play as a critical form of literacy, not a casual luxury.

As you begin the transformation of integrating more play into your teaching practice, understand that significant changes will occur, and your reaction to them will make or break the sustainability of play in your classroom. Take these changes into consideration and see them for what they are: joyful, authentic learning that embodies Dream Culture. Students will let their guard down; they will open to new experiences; they will self-police their behavior less because they feel freer.

This is not to say that we should not maintain an organizational structure to the class, but we cannot punish normative joyful behaviors of our students. Perhaps we have gotten too adjusted to a school environment of forced student stoicism, but we must remember that when students—and, frankly, adults—are authentically learning, it is often noisy and slightly chaotic, and that's OK.

Prepare yourself with a mindset tuned to the change that will take place and have a conversation with your students about what you are trying to accomplish. They may be skeptical at first because they are not used to being asked their opinion on creating classroom environments. But I assure you that once they trust your motives, they'll work with you to construct a joyful yet highly functional learning environment.

When things inevitably fail to go as planned, problem-solve with your students before making any knee-jerk decisions that betray their trust. This is the essence of cogenerative dialogues and cosmopolitanism in the classroom, as an open teacher and her students' communication become integral to the success of class culture.

If we value the imagination and see the value in young people dreaming themselves into STEM professions, we must give them access to spaces that trigger the imagination. If we place ourselves in spaces that ignite the spirit and activate imagination, something is triggered within. I have become increasingly convinced that human beings create space for what matters to them. The colors you choose for the walls and what you place on these walls are extensions of you. This connection we have to our environment or space is often presented as a one-way relationship. I suggest that the walls and the space speak back to us as well. Our environments are shrines to our values and representations of our worldview. As such, our classroom environment should reflect the value of diversity, community, imagination, creativity, and collaboration—it should emphasize the life-changing potential of our dreams.

Creating environments of play is one of the most underrated yet highly effective ways to begin constructing a Dream Culture in your classroom. It signals to students that they can show their authentic selves. This enables their stress response to be put at ease, so they are more fully present for learning, experiencing, and, yes, dreaming.

It is important, of course, to remember that humanity is beautifully messy—nothing about us is perfect, and assuming we should be perfect is unrealistic. We will stumble. We will make mistakes. We will be upset with ourselves, our students, our administration, and our colleagues when we fall short of our espoused values. An important part of developing and codifying a Dream Culture is granting ourselves and others the grace to be joyfully messy and boldly inquisitive. This is the only way we reconcile and move forward in building a lasting Dream Culture.

This is not an immediate process—I have no solutions that can be brought into existence without understanding and internalizing the necessary work involved. A Dream Culture is something that absolutely can be built everywhere, but it requires us to recognize both its power and its fragility. One cannot hope to build a lasting home on a foundation that has not first been carefully prepared and leveled. Without an earnest and genuine effort on our part to look inward, any Dream Culture we hope to create will be unsustainable. Without a willingness to let kids play—to discover and create on their own terms—any Dream Culture we build will be disingenuous. Yes, these are challenges. But before dismissing Dream Culture as too difficult or time consuming, consider the alternative. What happens when students stop dreaming and start merely conforming? What happens when all that is left in our STEM classrooms is trauma? Or isolation? Or feelings of deficiency and inadequacy?

The short answer is, we all suffer.

The longer answer is that creativity is stunted. Possibilities are squandered, and our collective potential is wasted. People are excluded from opportunity. And, bit by bit, we all lose hope.

Together, let's work to avoid this outcome. Let's activate our students' ability to dream and see beyond the boundaries created in the traditional, assessment-based classroom. We as educators must have an idea or a vision, take a risk in bringing it to young people, and then begin the work of helping them act on that vision in a way that moves it from imagination to reality. In the process of bringing imagination to life, the dream has to be communicated with those who share the same physical space. Then students must be motivated to work, create, and make in a way that goes beyond the norm. In the classroom—particularly when an educator can introduce young people to the beauty in a mathematical equation or scientific concept through a shared and joyous process—the personal connection begins. When joy meets a grand and shared vision and gets coupled with individual hard work and talent, the ingredients for a true Dream Culture exist.

Dream

TAKEAWAYS

- Too often, STEM classrooms are environments where young people are forced to learn. Students are disengaged and disinterested, and they respond with anger or frustration. The disengagement of our children from STEM must be corrected.

- In order to improve the conditions of STEM and learning in the US, we must first acknowledge and sit in the disaster we have created. Without reckoning with our mismanagement of students' dreams and potential, we cannot improve STEM.

- Allowing ourselves and our students the space for introspection and to reconnect with our values sets the foundation for creating a Dream Culture. The ability to reflect on an interaction with a student or to understand that something about your classroom culture feels out of step is a core attribute of a great educator.

- Play is a critical form of literacy, not a casual luxury. Creating environments of play is one of the most underrated yet highly effective ways to construct a Dream Culture. It signals to students that they can show their authentic selves, enabling them to be more fully present for learning, experiencing, and dreaming.

- A Dream Culture can be built everywhere, but it requires us to recognize both its power and its fragility. We will make mistakes. We will be upset when we fall short of our espoused values. An important part of developing a Dream Culture is acknowledging our imperfection and granting ourselves, as well as others, the grace to be human.

Appendix

Resource Library

We hope this curated list of resources supports you on the journey to embrace a *STEM, STEAM, Make, Dream* culture in your classroom and/or school. There are so many rich, diverse resources in the field—this list is in no way exhaustive. Please share your favorites on social media, using the hashtag #STEAMDream.

Organizations and Communities

- **The Calculus Project** is an initiative from Cambridge Education focused on increasing the number of students of color and low-income students who complete AP Calculus in high school. This initiative provides summer courses, tutoring sessions, and after-school study groups. https://www.camb-ed.com/americas/the-calculus-project
- **The Center for Gender Equity in Science and Technology** is a research unit from Arizona State University with the goal of creating an interdisciplinary, racially and ethnically diverse community of scholars, students, policymakers, and practitioners to explore, identify, critique, and create innovative scholarship relating to girls in STEM. The Center also offers culturally responsive programs for girls of color (e.g., African American, Native American, Latina, and Asian American) within STEM education. https://cgest.asu.edu/
- **Computer-Using Educators (CUE)** is a nonprofit organization focused on using technology to transform teaching and learning. https://cue.org/
- **DownCity Design** a nonprofit community design studio based in Providence, Rhode Island, that uses the tools of design to empower students, educators, and community members to improve their surroundings. DownCity Design offers free youth and professional development programs with the goal of using design to make a difference in the community. https://www.downcitydesign.org/

- **Girls Garage** is a nonprofit design and building organization offering after-school and summer programs in the realm of building, including carpentry, welding, architecture, engineering, and activist art, for female-identifying youth. Girls Garage programs also integrate technical skills, college and career guidance, and community leadership, offering a holistic experience. https://girlsgarage.org/
- **Girls Who Code** is an organization focused on closing the gender gap in the tech industry. It offers clubs, over eighty-five thousand programs, online resources, and more to encourage girls from diverse backgrounds to explore future careers in technology. https://girlswhocode.com/
- **Hip Hop Ed** is a nonprofit educational organization that works to empower students by utilizing youth culture. Hip Hop Ed facilitates innovative educational programming in schools and curates events, including an annual conference, that integrate the intersections of youth culture, education, and various industries. #HipHopEd, https://hiphoped.com/
- **If/Then** is dedicated to advancing and uplifting women in STEM, doing so through funding, cross-sector partnerships, and improving media portrayals of women in STEM fields. https://www.ifthenshecan.org/
- **Indigenous Education Tools**, part of the Building Capacity & Cultivating Innovation: Learning Agendas in Native Education (BCCI) project, develops resources and practices to improve Native student success in education. http://indigenouseducationtools.org/
- **The International Society for Technology in Education (ISTE)** is made up of educators dedicated to using technology as a tool for transformation and innovation in education, as well as a solution to obstacles. https://iste.org/
- **Instructables** is a site of thousands of projects (circuits, cooking, craft, building, and more) shared by a community of makers, innovators, and teachers. https://www.instructables.com/circuits/
- **Khan Academy** is a nonprofit organization offering free instructional videos across disciplines (including math, science, and computing) for grades K–12 and beyond. https://www.khanacademy.org/
- **The K12 Lab Network** is a program from the Stanford d.school specifically aimed at elementary and secondary educators. With this program, the d.school offers workshops, resources, and tools for educators, with the goal of eliminating opportunity

gaps in K–12 education. https://dschool.stanford.edu/programs/
k12-lab-network

- **Lincoln Center** is the world's leading presenter of superb artistic programming, and a national leader in arts and education and community relations. http://lincolncenter.org
- **The National Council of Teachers of Mathematics (NCTM)** is the world's largest education organization focused on mathematics. https://www.nctm.org/
- **The National Science Teaching Association (NSTA)** is an organization of science teachers, and supervisors, administrators, scientists, business and industry representatives, and more, dedicated to promoting excellence and innovation in science teaching and learning. https://www.nsta.org/
- **PBLWorks** is an organization from the Buck Institute for Education serving K–12 educators with the goal of bringing project based learning to all students. https://www.pblworks.org/
- **The Practice Space** is an organization that teaches youth and adults in the San Francisco area how to improve their communication skills. Through a variety of trainings (camps, school-based programs, and so on), the Practice Space aims to create a fun and safe space to build effective and inclusive communication. https://www.practice-space.org/
- **The Stanford University d.school** is focused on using design thinking principles to make change. Fundamental to this school are the beliefs that design should be accessible to all and that diversity leads to more creativity and better design. https://dschool.stanford.edu/
- **Science Genius** is an initiative from Hip Hop Ed dedicated to empowering students to engage in the wonder of science through hip-hop music and culture. As part of the initiative, students work independently and collaboratively to create science-themed raps and songs to enter into competition. https://hiphoped.com/science-genius/
- **STEMbassy** is a STEM communication organization, gathering individuals from all STEM fields to discuss science, technology, engineering, and mathematics in the context of politics, culture, and social issues. https://www.stembassy.org/
- **Teach Engineering** is a free STEM K–12 curriculum, covering a wide range of topics, including algebra, life sciences, physics, and science and technology. https://www.teachengineering.org/

- **Tinkerlab** is a blog full of hands-on art and science projects for preK–5 children. https://tinkerlab.com/
- **YouCubed**, a nonprofit organization from Stanford University, offers free K–12 math resources for educators and parents as well as affordable professional learning with the goal of using a growth mindset to improve mathematics success for all students. https://www.youcubed.org/

Apps and Tech Tools

- **Flocabulary** provides engaging videos that teach lessons in a range of subjects through hip-hop. Accompanying each video are interactive vocabulary cards, vocabulary games, reading passages, quizzes, and a Lyric Lab, which allows students to generate raps of their own. https://www.flocabulary.com/
- **GLOBE Observer** is an app that enables students to join an international network of citizen and professional scientists studying Earth and the global environment. Users submit photographs and observations about their environment to share with NASA and other scientists globally, contributing important scientific data. https://observer.globe.gov/en/about/get-the-app
- **Make Music Count** is an app from Marcus Blackwell for students in grades 3–12 that teaches math lessons through the playing of popular songs on a virtual piano. https://makemusiccount.com/
- **Scratch** is an app developed by MIT that allows students (ages 8–13) to learn the fundamentals of coding through the creation of interactive stories, games, and animations. https://scratch.mit.edu/
- **Prodigy Math** is a program that engages students (grades K–8) in the Prodigy Math Game world, where they use math to complete epic quests. https://www.prodigygame.com/main-en/

Books

- *Awesome Engineering Activities for Kids: 50+ Exciting STEAM Projects to Design and Build* by Christina Schul offers over fifty engineering activities for children ages 5–10.
- *The Art of Curiosity: 50 Visionary Artists, Scientists, Poets, Makers & Dreamers Who Are Changing the Way We See Our World* by Exploratorium is a resource in which fifty of the world's most creative people share the ways they've been inspired by the Exploratorium to change the world, including science and education.

- *The Art of Tinkering: Meet 150+ Makers Working at the Intersection of Art, Science & Technology* by Karen Wilkinson and Mike Petrich is a resource from the Exploratorium that shares stories from over 150 makers who celebrate the art of tinkering.
- *Girls Garage: How to Use Any Tool, Tackle Any Project, and Build the World You Want to See* by Emily Pilloton is a how-to full of guidance, projects, and stories about building, including carpentry, home repair, and DIY projects.
- *Invent to Learn: Making, Tinkering, and Engineering in the Classroom, Second Edition* by Sylvia Libow Martinez and Gary Stager is a practical guide for K–12 educators on how to bring the maker movement into the classroom. Eliminating the distinction between art and science, this resource supports teachers with the how and why of bringing making into education.
- *Make Space: How to Set the Stage for Creative Collaboration* by Scott Doorley and Scott Witthoft is based on work by the Stanford University d.school and its Environments Collaborative Initiative. Make Space explores how intentionally designed environments can increase creativity, communication, and innovation.

Events

- **Constructing Modern Knowledge** is an annual interactive conference focused on using computing and technology in the service of improving education and outcomes for all students. https://constructingmodernknowledge.com/
- The **Maker Faire** is a family-friendly event in San Francisco and New York, with independent mini-Faires occurring worldwide. This celebration of the maker movement brings together makers, creators, educators, engineers, and much more. https://makerfaire.com/
- The **SXSW EDU** is an annual conference and festival that gathers a community of educators, nonprofit organizations, students, and others with the goal of increasing innovation in education. https://www.sxswedu.com/
- **STEAMnasium** is an event presented by the Teachers College of Columbia University and hosted by faculty and students from the Mathematics, Science, and Technology Department. This event offers interactive stations for all things STEAM. https://steam.tc.columbia.edu/

Glossary

We view this glossary as an invitation to a conversation—with the belief that language has the power to both unify us and to form community. By sharing these key words in this resource, we hope to contribute to a common language that supports us as we're traveling on this journey together.

Culturally relevant pedagogy

A pedagogical and philosophical framework that focuses on numerous aspects of student achievement and encourages students to maintain their cultural identities. This includes calling on students to challenge societal inequalities.

Identity

Characteristics defining a person, shaped by the social and cultural environment.

Implicit bias

Unconscious feelings, beliefs, or understandings, including racial and cultural stereotypes, that affect perceptions of others.

Iteration

A new version of a product or software, intended as an improvement on previous versions.

Maker

A person who makes things.

Maker identity

The identity taken on by someone within the maker movement, related to the things they make.

Maker mindset

The idea that one has the agency and ability to creatively solve problems through critical thinking, collaboration, and communication.

Metacommunication

Nonverbal cues such as tone of voice, body language, and facial expressions that communicate how a message is meant to be interpreted. (This term was coined by Gregory Bateson.)

Microaggressions

Behaviors that occur in day-to-day interactions that reveal bias toward individuals belonging to marginalized groups.

Mirror neurons

A class of neurons that fire both when an individual displays an action and when that person observes another engaging in the same action. These neurons are an important aspect of human society, as they enable individuals to reflect and understand the body language, expressions, and emotions of others.

Play

The act of engaging in an activity for enjoyment rather than as a means to an end.

Project based learning (PBL)

A teaching method in which students are engaged in relevant, real-world projects.

Prototype

A preliminary model of an idea created for the purpose of testing the design and concept, to be improved on for final design.

Reality pedagogy

A teaching method that focuses on the cultural understandings of students within a particular social space, such as a science classroom. This method consists of the following five characteristics: cogenerative dialogues, coteaching, cosmopolitanism, context, and content.

Social entrepreneurship

A process in which individuals create products or services to address a societal need, including poverty, human rights, education, and sustainability.

User experience

The experience an individual has when using a product.

Resource: Essential Project Design Elements Checklist

Created by PBLWorks (www.pblworks.org)

Whatever form a project takes, it must meet these criteria to be gold standard PBL.

DOES THE PROJECT MEET THESE CRITERIA?			?

KEY KNOWLEDGE, UNDERSTANDING, AND SUCCESS SKILLS
The project is focused on teaching students key knowledge and understanding derived from standards and success skills including critical thinking/problem solving, collaboration, and self-management.

CHALLENGING PROBLEM OR QUESTION
The project is based on a meaningful problem to solve or a question to answer, at the appropriate level of challenge for students, which is operationalized by an open-ended, engaging driving question.

SUSTAINED INQUIRY
The project involves an active, in-depth process over time, in which students generate questions, find and use resources, ask further questions, and develop their own answers.

AUTHENTICITY
The project has a real-world context, uses real-world processes, tools, and quality standards, makes a real impact, and/or is connected to students' own concerns, interests, and identities.

STUDENT VOICE AND CHOICE
The project allows students to make some choices about the products they create, how they work, and how they use their time, guided by the teacher and depending on their age and PBL experience.

REFLECTION
The project provides opportunities for students to reflect on what and how they are learning, and on the project's design and implementation.

CRITIQUE AND REVISION
The project includes processes for students to give and receive feedback on their work, in order to revise their ideas and products or conduct further inquiry.

PUBLIC PRODUCT
The project requires students to demonstrate what they learn by creating a product that is presented or offered to people beyond the classroom.

Activities

Activity 1

PAPER-MODEL MAKING CHALLENGES

Created by Girls Garage (girlsgarage.org)

PURPOSE

This workshop activity from Girls Garage helps develop a builder's mindset. In this quick-fire hands-on workshop, participants complete a series of paper model-making exercises to flex their maker muscles. We also use exercises like these as "creative calisthenics" to engage different creative tactics for our projects. You can try out these activities yourself using common materials you have at home, and we recommend you complete them in the order listed here. Each prompt represents a different aspect of the builder's mindset that will challenge your visual and physical creativity.

GROUPING

Individual

MATERIALS

- Paper, card stock, and/or cardboard
- Scissors
- Tape

DIRECTIONS

Challenge 1: Production

In five minutes, make as many differently shaped paper models as you can! Whatever you do, keep your hands moving. The only requirement is that your models be three-dimensional and use two or more individual components of paper or cardboard. (In other words, you can't just bend or crumple one piece of paper). There's no requirement for what they look like or what size they are.

Challenge 2: Concept

We're inspired by the raw conceptualism of Richard Serra's large steel sculptures. Years ago, he wrote a list of verbs and action words to spark his initial form-making, called *Verblist*. (Search online for this; it's also viewable on MOMA's website, https://www.moma.org/collection/works/152793.) For this second paper modeling challenge, pick a verb like *to curve*, *to collect*, *to join*, or *to scatter*, and in two minutes, make a model that represents it, either literally or conceptually. Do as many iterations with as many words as you want!

Challenge 3: Purpose

In six minutes, build a supporting structure to showcase and hold one of the models you've built in the previous exercises (pick your favorite!). Take time to consider the craft and engineering of the structure and the connection between the sculpture and the model itself.

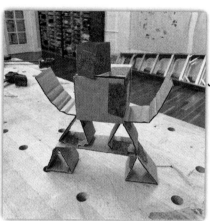

Activity 2

MOOD MAPPING

Created by DownCity Design (downcitydesign.org)

PURPOSE

Often when we're seeking to transform a space or place, we focus more on noticing the problems we see, rather than on what's already working well. Mapping *all* the moods associated with a place can help us figure out how best to identify and address the challenges present there. This activity helps develop empathy and observation skills.

GROUPING

Small groups of 3–6 people

MATERIALS

- Paper
- Assorted colored markers

DIRECTIONS

Get Out There

In small groups, walk slowly through a building or neighborhood you're hoping to improve. As you go, pay attention to how the environment affects what you're feeling—from room to room, street to street, block to block.

Map It

Working as a group, use different colored markers to represent shifting moods on your map. Does one block or room feel particularly lonely? Trace it in black. Is another lively and vibrant? Mark it with a warm color, like red. Make notes on your map with all of the factors that contribute to the moods you've identified. What makes one block lonely—are there a lot of parking lots or abandoned buildings? Are there no street lights? What makes another block vibrant—are there places for people to gather and play? List as many assets and problems as you can, and mark them in the appropriate places on your map.

Pin It Up

Back in your classroom, pin up and compare all the groups' maps. Identify the areas that your group finds problematic and the areas that are working well. Where do they overlap?

Plan It Out

Make a list of possible places for intervention—sites that will allow you to make the most of the great stuff that exists, while minimizing the negative elements. Once you've figured out what issues you'd like to address as a group, you're ready to move on to exploring possible solutions!

Activity 3

SHARK TANK—SOCIAL ENTREPRENEURSHIP

Created by Mary Beth Hertz (twitter.com/mbteach)

PURPOSE

This is a really hard but rewarding project. Students learn how to really think through solving societal issues in a concrete, financially sustainable way and also come to agreement on how to solve these issues and run their businesses. The project is "sink or swim," to model how real businesses work—they require teamwork and accountability. Each business has a CEO and other specific roles within the company that students self-organize around in the same way that any real business would need to operate.

GROUPING

Self-organized teams

MATERIALS

Templates (see directions)

DIRECTIONS

Whole-Class Brainstorm

First, the whole class brainstorms a number of societal issues that they think need solving, such as homelessness, hunger, and the environment. Students then sit in groups to discuss each larger issue and identify specific challenges tied to these issues. For instance, lack of job opportunities for the homeless or carbon emissions from vehicles that lead to air pollution.

Self-Organize and Form Businesses

Students self-organize in groups around these larger issues and then branch off around specific challenges that they want to address to form their business. Share a business planning document (many are available for free online) so that the students may start pulling together the goals and purpose of their business, including researching the competition.

Identify the Business Type

Support each group as they fine-tune their idea and identify how they will make money. Some groups may decide to form a nonprofit. Others will likely be interested in traditional "social entrepreneurship" businesses.

Create the Business Model

Students work on a business plan template, researching their target audience, identifying the competition, and figuring out how their business will be competitive, completing a SWOT (strengths, weaknesses, opportunities, threats) analysis to assess the viability of their business model and to identify internal and external threats to their business.

Write the Pitch

Support teams as they refine their business plan and prepare to pitch their business to "sharks," who will decide whether their company is worth investing in.

Recruit "Sharks" for the Tank

Recruit sharks from members of the school community or beyond the school walls. You may want to have the shark team assess the business pitches with a rubric (also easily found online by searching on "Shark Tank Rubric").

Create Assets

The teams must create assets for their business, including a logo, a short promotional video (no more than two minutes), a prototype of some kind, marketing materials, and a business plan.

Activity 4

ANALYZING A SCIENCE IDENTITY

> **Created by Neal Schick (twitter.com/nealpaulschick)**

PURPOSE

If we want to be successful in embarking on a journey of teaching science, or any subject matter, to students, we have to break the deficit-based narratives that many of our students have internalized. The biggest factor in interrupting the deficit mindsets we often see in our students is to get them to think about and confront those mindsets. We must show students that the barrier to their success is not due to a deficit of skill, but because of a mental and emotional mindset created by a society that tells them they are not capable of being or thinking like scientists. This is important even if students don't go on to be professional scientists. The mindset this activity creates can help students be more interrogative about the world and guide them to developing scientific skill sets as they collect and share evidence. Setting up a classroom culture where students can break out of these deficit-based narratives enables students to start thinking and dreaming without limit.

GRADES

6–12 (This activity can also be adapted to meet the needs of any grade.)

GROUPING

Whole class

MATERIALS

Create a slide show of 10–15 photos of a diverse range of scientists (past and contemporary, spanning gender, race, etc.) Use images that vary in context, so that some feature obvious scientific themes while others do not. (Some scientists might be pictured in a lab, for example, while others might be pictured in a more casual setting.) Some individuals you might feature include Neil deGrasse Tyson, Dr. Lynn Margulis, Dr. Chris Emdin, Dr. Mae Jemison, Dr. Percy Julian, and Thomas Edison.

TIME

One 45- to 50-minute class period, though the conversation may warrant extended discussion

DIRECTIONS

1. Begin by asking students to draw a scientist and respond to the following prompt: *When you think about an image of a scientist working, what does that mean to you?* Then have students share their thinking. Students will likely describe a scientist in the stereotypical sense—as a white man with crazy hair and glasses working in a lab. This discussion does not need to be elaborate, but is just meant as a way to get these images in students' minds before the next step.

2. Using the slide show created per the Materials list, show the first image. Ask students to write down three things:
   - What do you think is this person's career?
   - What observations are you making from the photo that lead you to think this?
   - Do you think this person does something that involves science? Yes or no?

   You may choose to post these questions on the board or have them preprepared on a handout. After showing each slide, encourage students to share their thinking. Know that at this stage, students may not engage in deep discussion as they share their thinking.

   ### Examples of Student Thinking

   (Regarding a photo of Dr. Lynn Margulis) "I think she's a gardener."
   (Regarding a photo of Dr. Percy Julian) "He must be an assistant because he is delivering a message."

3. When you have worked through the slide show once, show each photo again, this time engaging students in a discussion about their thinking. Have them discuss each person and the evidence they collected from the image to support their thinking. Finally, have the class vote for whether or not they think the person in the photo is a scientist. You'll notice students start to engage in a vibrant debate on their opinions; they'll use the evidence they collected to argue in a scientific manner—identifying the common denominators they see in each photo.

4. After going through all the photos a second time, encourage students to think about which images had the highest number of votes cast for yes, meaning the person pictured is a scientist. During this discussion, students will start to see the trends in their voting. They'll being to notice that the people who received the most yes votes were all white and were all men. Ask questions such as *Why do you think these trends emerge? Why do we believe these things? Why are these deep-seated narratives in our head?* to encourage students to think about the implicit bias that influenced their decisions.
   Note: Realizing their own implicit bias may make some students feel bad. It is critical at this moment to explain that implicit bias is unconscious and held by everyone. For further ideas on exploring

implicit bias, consider introducing Project Implicit, a nonprofit organization dedicated to researching implicit social cognition (https://implicit.harvard.edu/implicit/).

5. After discussing some of these questions, ask students to write down how they would identify themselves. Then have students close their eyes and silently envision the career paths of individuals that identify as being similar to themselves. Have students use their observations of the world to come up with as many careers as they can. Again, here you'll notice some trends. White male students often think of jobs such as accountant, engineer, doctor, president, attorney general, senator, and the like, whereas female students, particularly female students of color, may list jobs such as caretaker, teacher, nurse, secretary, hairdresser, babysitter, and so on. Some students will think of jobs that push against the grain, which is amazing, but the aforementioned patterns will still emerge. Use this opportunity to talk about where these ideas come from and whether they're actually a manifestation of one's capability or whether they're caused by internalized narratives. Eventually, students will come to the conclusion that these narratives about who and what they can be have no substance. It's important to emphasize that these narratives are socially fabricated and constructed and that it's your job (yours and your students' together) to break these narratives. Then you can discuss students' values and the impacts they want to have on the world.

6. If necessary, make connections to narratives that go beyond your class. For example, one year I presented my students with an article about young people that stated that they had no respect for authority and were a menace to society. I asked my students whom they thought this article was referring to, and they were shocked to learn that it was in fact describing a group of college students acting out after their team lost a game. It defied what the students thought of upper-middle-class college students and helped them see that the narratives we internalize aren't always true.

Tip: Be sure to enter this activity wanting to authentically engage in the conversation. It is helpful to bring your own experiences with a deficit-based narrative to the discussion. If you're not ready for that, an alternative is to share someone else's story. Neil deGrasse Tyson has a really powerful video in which he shares his own story of being told he wasn't smart in school and how he persisted despite that.

REFLECTION QUESTIONS

- What are three things that stood out to you that you want to contribute to our continued conversation?

- What are two things that produced a moment of pause for you that you want to further interrogate but don't know how to bring up in conversation?
- What is one thing you can take away and share with someone who was not part of this discussion?

Dr. Ayanna Howard

Dr. Michael Kobrick

George Washington Carver

Dr. Elvia Niebla

Dr. N. Christina Hsu

Thomas Edison

Dr. Claudia Alexander

Dr. Chris Emdin

Activity 5

WHAT CAN TOY BUILDING BRICKS TELL US ABOUT SCIENCE?

Created by Neal Schick (twitter.com/nealpaulschick)

PURPOSE

A critical element of scientific literacy is that human society—and the scientific progress that has assisted it—is a construction built on collaboration. Diverse viewpoints and perspectives are essential to our progress because scientific discovery is too great an endeavor for one person to accomplish alone. This activity underscores this idea, engaging students in a way that authentically and organically reveals this truth.

GROUPING

Students are purposely never given the specifics on this. This activity is initially framed to "sound" like an individual one, but with the intent that organic cooperation sprouts up and spreads as students progress through it, exchanging ideas and working together.

MATERIALS

Building bricks (100 per student; LEGO® bricks work well for this)

■ It's best to give identical sets of building bricks to every student—this reinforces how limitless unique configurations can originate from the same source material.
■ Ensure diversity within the 100 bricks to both challenge students and give a rich mix of 1×1, 2×2, 3×2, 4×2, etc. bricks.

DIRECTIONS

For the Student

All 100 bricks must be used. The activity is over once this has been achieved for all brick sets in the class.

For the Teacher

The most challenging but important aspect of this activity is that you give no additional directions than what is stated above for students. If they ask procedural questions, reiterate the directions above. This can be exceptionally difficult for many teachers, as students will likely express frustration that the directions are not more specific. This is intentional—allow students to constructively struggle through this.

As students work, feel free to circulate through the class and ask open probing questions of students. Questions should not be expecting a "correct" answer but should be designed to better understand the complete picture of students' thought processes. Examples could include the following:

- "I see you are _____. What made you think to do that?"
- "I hear you are feeling frustration about using all the 1 × 1 bricks. What is causing the frustration, and how might you problem-solve this?"

Sooner or later, students will likely begin asking if they can start trading bricks or collaborating with one another. When these questions start popping up, point students back to the directions and ask whether their proposed idea will satisfy the criteria given. For example:

- "I heard you ask if you could exchange four of your 2 × 2 bricks for four of your classmate's 3 × 2 bricks. Looking at the directions for the activity, will this trade still allow you to satisfy the criteria?"
- "I heard you ask if you could combine your bricks with your classmate's bricks to build one structure between the two of you. Looking at the directions for the activity, will this still allow you to satisfy the criteria?"

When students respond to your probing questions, it is important not to stop with a simple yes-no answer. Ask follow-up questions to get them to elaborate on their reasoning. If they say no, ask them what specific criteria they would not be meeting. If they say yes, ask them to explain why their new cooperation would still allow the criteria to be met.

Final results will vary between classes and the diversity of students in each, but there will almost always be some level of cooperation that arises if the teacher allows it to organically occur. Discuss this with students in reflection afterward and draw out why the cooperation took place. Ask what sparked the idea to cooperate in the first place and how students viewed the activity before, versus after, trading and collaboration began to occur. In many ways, this reflects the cultures of cooperation that must exist for science to be conducted effectively. Information must be shared, and problem solving is almost always more effective when people with different perspectives and world experiences collaborate.

Activity 6

WATER IN STORYDRAWING

Created by Indigenous STEAM (https://indigenoussteam.org/)

PURPOSE

Use this activity to focus your attention on your relationship with waters around you. Indigenous people have intimate relationships with the water of our planet, Mother Earth. Anishinaabe peoples express gratitude for relations with water through ceremony and song, and other Indigenous communities have varying protocols for recognizing water as relation. Water stories have been shared in Indigenous communities across generations to maintain teachings and relationships. Using stories, you can understand water as a relative and build relationships toward a positive future. During this activity, you will reflect on your favorite memories visiting waters and share those memories through a story picture.

GROUPING

Family and individual

MATERIALS

Various

DIRECTIONS

Talk about important, fun, or memorable experiences that your family has had with water.

Make a picture of a favorite memory from your time with water, or from water's perspective. This could be water you visited or water in the home. What stories did water share? Were there human, plant, animal, or other relatives with water? Why did you select this memory?

Tell, write, or record the story and share as a family.

Roles, Relations, Responsibilities, and Gifts

- Imagine how water you remembered was like in the past and future; what may be different or the same?
- Consider the gifts received when you visit the water and what can be offered in return.
- Discuss the current risks water faces, such as pollution, being owned, and climate change. How can humans and more-than-humans help minimize these risks?
- How are the relatives in your picture related? Are there beings or relationships that aren't visible?

Learning Across Generations and with Other Families

- Take time to hear the ideas from everyone in your family. What do you learn from each other? What are the different perspectives the youngest and oldest children bring?
- Talk with relatives, friends, and elders about your memories of the water. What do they know, remember, or imagine about that place? What stories do they have with water?
- Share your story with family and friends. Ask them to share stories in return.

Supporting Learning and Well-Being

- Consider the water as a relative to support your sense of security. How do you feel when you think about visiting water? What relationships have been developed?
- Ask family and friends what memories they've made with water. How have they been good relatives to water?
- While walking with your family, look for places with water. What behaviors do you see the water taking on? How do interactions with land and beings shape the water? Can you communicate this in your art?
- Look at pictures of Indigenous art. How or where do you see water in these images? Do they remind you of your family stories and experiences?

Making Relations with Land and Water

- Look back at the picture and consider who is represented in the place surrounding the water. Add anything from your memories or imagination that might be missing.
- What does this place look like during other seasons? Consider how and why the water and this place change across seasons.
- Consider ways to strengthen relationships with water in that place. How might we strengthen relations with water when we're not there?

Making Connections with Stories

- Share stories of other waters you have visited as a family.
- Imagine stories about water in different places.
- Tell or listen to stories and songs from your community about water.
- Search online with these keywords: "Nibi Song (Anishinaabe)," and for another story: "Ojibwe Flood Story."

Decolonization, Resurgence, and Good Relations

- Consider social movements around water sovereignty across our extended kin communities (#NoDAPL, #WaterIsLife, #ShutDownLine5, Flint Water Crisis) and ways local leaders have worked for change (e.g., Grandmother Josephine Mandamin, Billy Frank Jr., Senator John McCoy, and Black Lives Matter organizers).

- Discuss ways that relationships with water work to secure positive Indigenous futures and connect as coconspirators with extended kin, particularly between and within Indigenous and Black communities.
- Discuss who has access to water and who doesn't. How has climate change and corporate influence changed relationships with water? What efforts of activism can we take to secure healthy waters?
- Talk about ways to take care of the water every day. Consider visiting the water to offer gifts and build strong relationships.

Notes

Chapter 1

1. Shen Lu and Katie Hunt, "China's 'Good Will Hunting?' Migrant Worker Solves Complex Math Problem," CNN, July 17, 2016, https://www.cnn .com/2016/07/17/asia/china-migrant-worker-good-will-hunting/index .html.

Chapter 6

1. Y. Kim, K. Edouard, K. Aderfer, and B. K. Smith, "Making Culture, " 2019, https://drexel.edu/excite/engagement/learning-innovation /making-culture-report/.
2. T. Bajarin, "Maker Faire: Why the Maker Movement Is Important to America's Future," May 19, 2014, https://time.com/104210/maker -faire-maker-movement/.
3. Kim et al., "Making Culture."
4. "Making Culture."

Chapter 7

1. T. Bajarin, "Maker Faire: Why the Maker Movement Is Important to America's Future," May 19, 2014, https://time.com/104210/maker -faire-maker-movement/.
2. Y. Kim, K. Edouard, K. Aderfer, and B. K. Smith, "Making Culture, " 2019, https://drexel.edu/excite/engagement/learning-innovation /making-culture-report/.

Chapter 9

1. C. Jason Throop and Charles D. Laughlin, "Ritual, Collective Effervescence and the Categories: Toward a Neo-Durkheimian Model of the Nature of Human Consciousness, Feeling and Understanding," *Journal of Ritual Studies* (2002): 40–63.